PATTERNS FOR SOFT TOYS

This book is dedicated to my goddaughters
Jane and Sally

PATTERNS FOR SOFT TOYS

Applying soft toy techniques

ENID
ANDERSON

B.T. BATSFORD LTD, LONDON

ACKNOWLEDGEMENTS

My sincere thanks go to the following people: Ray Banks of Windsor Spice Studios for photographing all the toy models; Tina Stubbs who typed the manuscript; Valerie Dawson for her valuable help with machining the dolls' clothes; June Arnold for the machine embroidery and assistance in designing some items; Saflon Ltd, Leicester, who kindly supplied all the toy fillings for the original models; Margaret Annand of Mea Crafts for checking the manuscript; Simon Young of *The Artworker* for his advice on graphic art materials, and lastly to my family, without whose support none of my craft ventures would be possible.

By the same author:

The Great Soft Toy Cat and Kitten Book (1981)
Crafts and the Disabled (1982)
The Techniques of Soft Toymaking (1982)

ISBN 0 7134 4553 X

Typeset by Tek-Art Ltd, Kent
and printed in Great Britain by
R.J. Acford
Chichester, Sussex
for the publishers
B.T. Batsford Ltd
4 Fitzhardinge Street
London W1H 0AH

CONTENTS

INTRODUCTION

This is the companion volume to *The Techniques of Soft Toymaking*, published by Batsford in 1982. So many techniques were devised and researched for this first book that the restricted size made it impossible to include toy patterns for the reader to use as an alternative to designing their own soft toys.

Patterns for Soft Toys shows how to apply some of the techniques learned in the previous book, with a wide selection of soft toy designs to make this possible. This is, therefore, not a random collection of soft toy patterns. Each one is not only designed to incorporate the previously learned techniques, but is also graded according to the degree of difficulty, so that, by the end of the book; the reader should be, if not already, an accomplished toymaker. The grading of a pattern is, of course, relative to the expertise of the individual toymaker, and therefore the grades given to the patterns are purely suggested guidelines.

The contents, comprising 44 items in 26 projects, should be useful to all toymakers at whatever level, whether they are students learning the subject, teachers already established in the craft of toymaking or people making toys in a domestic capacity.

Whilst I have presented you with a selection of soft toy patterns, I do hope that this will not restrict you only to making toys from other people's designs. To design your own toys is so exciting and fulfilling, and not nearly as difficult as might be imagined; so be adventurous and, however basic your first design might be, do persevere, as you will find it so very rewarding.

GENERAL INSTRUCTIONS

At the back of the book is an appendix on the more general basic techniques of soft toymaking; for the specialized techniques it will be necessary to refer to *The Techniques of Soft Toymaking*.

PATTERN GRAPHS

The number on the caption lists of the pattern pieces refers to the numbers marked on the patterns, not to the order of the stages of work.

The pile line arrowing on the pattern layouts on the graphs may not be lined up as they will be when placed on the fabric at the cutting out stage; this is to enable the condensing of the pattern pieces on the graphs, thus providing room for a greater number of patterns in the book. To keep the annotations on the graph patterns to a minimum, thus enabling the pattern outlines to remain clear and easier to see for enlarging, certain variations in line styles have been used in the drawing of the patterns (see Diagram 1).

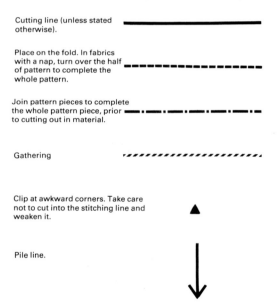

Cutting line (unless stated otherwise).

Place on the fold. In fabrics with a nap, turn over the half of pattern to complete the whole pattern.

Join pattern pieces to complete the whole pattern piece, prior to cutting out in material.

Gathering

Clip at awkward corners. Take care not to cut into the stitching line and weaken it.

Pile line.

Diagram 1   Graph markings

When pattern pieces are placed on the fold on the graphs to save space, there may not always be room to indicate that the base should be left open to both outside edges; similarly, when a pattern piece completely overlaps another on the graph layout, it may not be possible to indicate where the pattern

should be left open. Follow the written instructions carefully where it will state such necessary information. Refer to Diagram 2 when it is necessary to make a complete pattern piece.

On all graphs, except those indicated, one square = 2.5cm (1in).

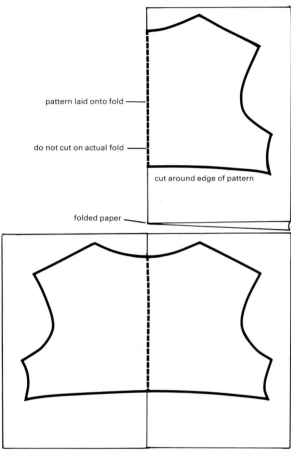

pattern laid onto fold

do not cut on actual fold

cut around edge of pattern

folded paper

paper opened out, remove pattern shape

Diagram 2   To make a complete pattern piece: enlarge the half pattern given and lay the edge marked 'on the fold' along the folded edge of another piece of paper. Cut around the outline but do not cut on the actual fold line. Unfold the paper to produce a full pattern piece.

ENLARGED PATTERNS

Once the patterns have been enlarged it is advisable to mount them on to card. Before starting to use the mounted pattern, check each pattern piece carefully to ensure that all the annotations have been added on to them, for example toy subject, pile line, number of pattern pieces required and so on.

Careful preparation at this stage will save considerable time later. A neatly fitting pattern produces a good start to a satisfactory end product; badly prepared patterns lead to misshapen toys, frustration and disappointment. Some of the smaller designs have been included in their actual sizes and not on a graph.

PATTERN INSTRUCTION LAYOUT

To enable the reader to see the development of the designs, and to learn the methods of approach to designing and the reasons for each subject choice, a design brief and an evaluation of design are given, where applicable. Any special techniques are listed and the choice of materials (if particularly relevant to the toy subject). If a special effect is required, the colouring and type of fabrics used will be given.

Each pattern is to a similar layout to enable the reader to progress from design to design with ease. Occasionally the structure of a toy design may require a variation in the making instructions, layout and the mode of presentation. It is a good idea to read through several patterns before starting to make the toys in this book, in order to see the method of instruction.

MATERIALS

Soft toymaking permits the usage of oddments of new material that might otherwise be discarded. However, whilst it is possible to use materials to hand rather than purchasing the exact colour required, there is sometimes a danger that the toymaker will be disappointed with the end product because it may not match the photographs in the book. Colouring is very important, and if the exact colours of the materials are given and the toymaker takes notice of the colour choice in relation to the design, it is then a learning area to assist in future toymaking.

Whilst material quantities have, wherever possible, been broken down into units to the minimum requirement to enable the reader to use materials already in stock, if purchasing the requirements for each toy, it is advisable in most cases to buy a larger quantity than is stated, especially on the smaller items. The reason for this is that it is most uneconomical to purchase small quantities of any materials. The larger the piece of material, the greater the proportional number of toys which can be made. Obviously there are exceptions to this rule, and it is for the reader to decide according to individual requirements.

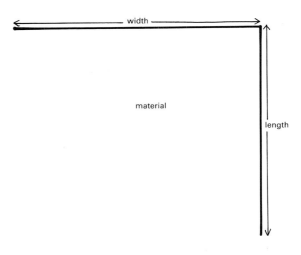

Diagram 3 The width and length measurements of a piece of material. Usually in patterns the material measurements are given width × length; on fur fabric the pile line would be the length measurement.

It is sometimes difficult for a student to arrive at the same pattern layout on the material quantity given as the designer, especially where fur fabric is involved; as a guide, the width measurement is usually given first, followed by the length requirement. In some patterns, mainly the dolls' clothes, the imperial conversions have been rounded up to the nearest amount.

CONSTRUCTION

A 0.7cm (¼in) seam allowance has been made on each pattern piece, unless otherwise stated. To save constant repetition and space, on each set of making instructions the following notes should be observed for each toy. After cutting out the pattern pieces in the desired materials, these should, for example in the case of limbs, first be pinned together in pairs and then stitched together, and the pins removed prior to turning to the right side or progressing to the next stage. The fur fabric toys should always be groomed on completion, taking care to tease out any pile caught in the seams and brushing in the direction of the pile line. Any ribbons or materials should be ironed prior to application to the toy.

The method of writing toymaking instructions in craft books is usually the personal choice of the author, often decided in consultation with the publisher. To the established toymaker any variations between designers pose few problems;

9

however, students new to the subject may find it helpful to have some facts explained before starting their toymaking. For example, 'hand cut four' means two pieces for each hand not four pieces for one hand. Sometimes in the making instructions any pattern parts may be listed in the singular, for example 'Hand. Place together in pairs.' The instructions then proceed to explain the construction of one hand and, when that is completed, then state 'make the other hand in the same way'. Other instructions may list the various pattern parts in the plural.

If you approach your toymaking in a slow, un-hurried manner, and work in a tidy way, fewer mistakes will occur. In the first volume, a section of the book was used to illustrate 'Utilizing a pattern to its fullest potential'. The subject chosen to do this was a rabbit. With a few alterations it became a wide range of toy subjects: a fur circle rabbit, a pram cover and matching hanging toys, a nightdress case, a double-ended toy, a jack-in-the-box, a stick puppet and a glove puppet with a pram and baby. At the request of readers of the previous volume, these rabbit patterns have been included, not as one complete project but as individual items using different design ideas. Do take note, however, of the relationship between these designs, and maybe you will be encouraged to make similar use of toy patterns you may already have.

EXAMPLE OF THE PATTERN LAYOUT AND EXPLANATION OF THE CONTENT

THE TOY'S TITLE

SIZE
The size of the toy subject

GRADING
Degree of difficulty

TECHNIQUES
Any new main techniques

DESIGN BRIEF
A brief description of the intended toy subject

EVALUATION OF DESIGN BRIEF
The approach to any design criteria and reasons for subject choice

DEVELOPMENT OF THE DESIGN
The progression to the finished toy

CHOICE OF MATERIALS
Any special material types required to achieve a particular effect

MATERIALS REQUIRED
Either the exact quantities of each material or, in the case of the small toys or smaller items where very little material amounts are required, the oddments needed

CONSTRUCTION
The making instructions

For ease of copying, the graphs have been reproduced at the fullest size possible; some have, therefore, been placed sideways on the page, as shown by the annotations.

1
FLAT STITCH AROUND DOLL

Figure 1. Flat stitch around doll

SIZE
Height 24.1cm (9½in)

GRADING
Easy

TECHNIQUES
Stitch around flat toy method

DESIGN BRIEF
A basic stitch around soft toy

EVALUATION OF DESIGN BRIEF
A stitch around toy requires a clear basic outline. The subject must be suitable for an even, all-over stuffing surface. The pattern given here can be used as a basis for many doll subjects, only requiring a change of body colouring and features.

MATERIALS REQUIRED

Basic doll body Felt measuring 40.6cm (16in) × 25.4cm (10in)

Features Small oddments of felt

Hair A piece of shaggy pile fur fabric 12.7cm (5in) long for around the doll's face, 5cm (2in) deep at either side of the head, curving to a depth of approximately 9cm (3½in) at the centre back of the head (looped wool could be used)

Trousers Cotton or similar material 20.4cm (8in) × 11.5cm (4½in); a piece of narrow elastic for the waist, 15.3cm (6in) long

Waistcoat Felt 20.4cm (8in) × 10.3cm (4in)

Neck bow A piece of narrow velvet ribbon 30.5cm (12in) long

Toy filling

CONSTRUCTION
Cut out the pattern pieces as listed

Body Fold the felt in half to measure 20.4cm (8in) × 25.4cm (10in). Pin to hold together. Mount the body pattern on to card and, using tailor's chalk, draw the pattern outline shape on to the felt. Remove the pattern and, using either a sewing machine or handstitching using a small backstitch, sew along the drawn outline, leaving a stuffing

11

Doll pattern pieces

1 Body: cut two in brown felt. The features comprise: two felt eyebrows in orange felt; two eye bases in white felt; two eye pupils in black felt; one 2cm (¾in) diameter circle of red felt for the nose, and one mouthpiece in orange felt with the centre removed to form the mouth.

2 Waistcoat front: cut two in felt. The curved inner line indicates the fold for the lapel.

3 Waistcoat back: cut one in felt.

4 Trousers: cut two in cotton or similar material.

12

opening at the top of the head. Cut out the toy near to the stitched outline, but not close enough to weaken the stitches. Do not turn the toy inside out.

Stuff the body firmly, but keep the flat image and avoid any bulges by making sure the toy filling is evenly distributed. Close the stuffing opening using ladder stitch.

Features To assist the placing of the features, pin the hair-piece into place at the sides of the head where indicated on the pattern. Cut out the features. The nose is a 2cm (¾in) diameter circle of felt, gathered around the outside edge then stuffed and the gathering stitches pulled up tightly to form a ball.

Pin the features on to the face and, when satisfied that the desired expression has been achieved, remove the pins and glue the eyebrows, eyes and mouth into place using a latex-based adhesive, for example Copydex. The nose is ladder stitched to the face.

Hair Remove the pins and ladder stitch around the outside edge of the shaggy pile fur fabric to the head, first from one side of the face to the other, and then continuing round the back of the head, until all edges on the hair-piece are securely stitched to the head. If there are any gaps in the stitching it may be necessary to stitch round the head piece a second time.

Trousers With the right sides of the material facing, stitch down both of the 11.5cm (4½in) side seams. To divide for the legs, cut a slit at the centre of the material from the bottom upwards towards the waist measuring 7.6cm (3in). Stitch the seams on either side of the slit together, front to back.

Turn a 1.3cm (½in) hem at the waist, leaving a small opening to thread with narrow elastic. Turn up a 0.7cm (¼in) hem at the bottom of the trouser legs; this should leave approximately 0.7cm (¼in) of each foot showing when the trousers are on the doll. Turn to the right side.

Waistcoat Stitch the shoulder seams together, fronts to the back for 2.5cm (1in). Stitch the side seams together from the lower edge each side for 2.5cm (1in), leaving the armholes open. Turn to the right side.

Fold the lapels back each side where indicated by the curved inner line on the pattern. The waistcoat can be left free without any fastenings, or, if preferred, small pieces of Velcro can be stitched or glued under one front piece of the waistcoat near the point and on to the under piece to secure the waistcoat to the doll's waist. It should be noted, however, that felt is only composed of impacted fibres and will therefore fray if constantly being pulled against any fastening.

2
HOBBY HORSE

HEAD SIZE
From the neck to the top of the ears 40.6cm (16in)

GRADING
Easy

TECHNIQUES
Application of a toy head to a pole or broom handle

DESIGN BRIEF
A simply constructed hobby horse without wheels

EVALUATION OF DESIGN BRIEF
The hobby horse has survived for many years, in medieval and Renaissance prints it is often depicted as a complete horse carved and attached to the end of a striped pole. Later it developed into a more simple head decorated with trimmings and ribbons with wheels and a crossbar to enable easy holding. During the nineteenth century it is said their popularity dwindled as the rocking horse came into being. Today we see many different hobby horse designs made in a variety of materials, for example hessian, felt, tweeds and many others. In contrast to these, fur fabric was chosen for this horse.

MATERIALS REQUIRED

Fur fabric 35.5cm (14in) × 71.2cm (28in); the pile line is the 71.2cm (28in) measurement

One pair of 18mm safety lock eyes

Mane One strip of shaggy pile fur fabric, measuring 76.2cm (30in) long × 10.3cm (4in) wide

Felt For the ear linings 15.3cm (6in) × 15.3cm (6in) Oddments of felt to use behind the eyes and for the eyelashes

Two 2.5cm (1in) diameter circles of black felt for the nostrils
Toy filling
One broom handle (these vary considerably in price and the most expensive are not necessarily the strongest)
Oddments of sheeting or strong tape to bind the top portion of the broom handle

Harness One puppy collar
Two puppy leads: these look most authentic, but, if unavailable, other mediums could be used, the

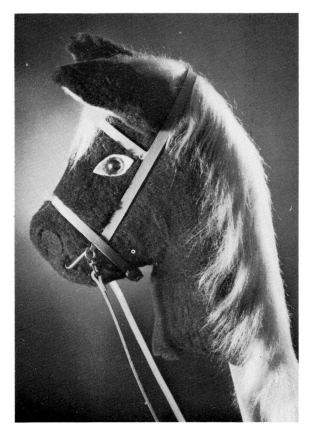

Figure 2. Hobby horse

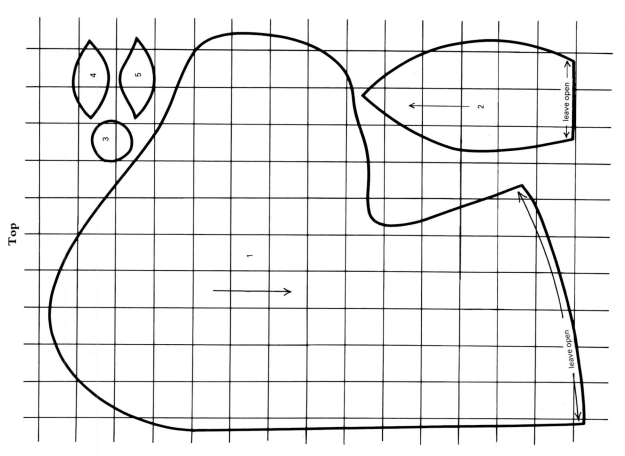

Top

leave open

leave open

4

5

3

2

1

Hobby horse pattern pieces

1 Head: cut two in fur fabric (one reversed).
2 Ears: cut two in fur fabric; cut two in felt for linings.
3 Nostrils: cut two in black or brown felt.
4 Eye bases: cut two in white felt.
5 Eyelids: cut two in felt to tone with the body fabric.

main consideration being that they must be strong
enough to withstand considerable wear

Copydex adhesive
Polyurethane clear varnish or non-toxic paint

CONSTRUCTION
Cut out the pattern pieces as listed.

Head Place the head pieces together, right sides
facing. Pin, then backstitch around the outside
edge, leaving the bottom straight edge open. Turn
to the right side and partially stuff from the nose to

just below the eye placing. Insert the safety lock
eyes, placing a felt eye base behind each eye. Stuff
the head firmly, omitting to stuff the neck.

Prepare the broom handle by rubbing smooth
with glass-paper and then either painting or
varnishing it. If preferred, the handle can be rubbed
down and polished with a good wax furniture
polish. When dry, cut strips of sheeting 5cm (2in)
wide, glue one end to the top of the broom handle
and bind tightly for approximately 30.5cm (12in)
down the handle; glue to fasten off. The binding
material should be fairly thick on the handle to
enable easy stitching of the head, and it may,
therefore, be necessary to bind a second time to
achieve this.

When it is completely dry, insert this bound end
into the horse's head, parallel to the back seam.
Stitch firmly through the fur fabric at the back of
the horse's head to the sheeting to secure both
together. This will hold the head firmly in place on
the broom handle. Stuff the rest of the head and the
neck very firmly, paying careful attention to the

area around the broom handle. Ladder stitch the straight seams at the base of the neck together; before closing, insert more filling, then finally close.

Mane With the pile direction on the mane piece going from the top of the head down the back of the head, pin the mane in place following the line of the back seam, then ladder stitch down both sides of the mane to attach it to the horse's head. Stitch across the mane at the forehead. The mane is longer than the back of the horse's head. The seams on the excess mane are ladder stitched together and left hanging.

Ears With right sides facing, place together in pairs one fur fabric and one felt lining for each ear; pin then stitch around the outside edge of each ear, leaving the bottom straight edges open. Turn to the right side. Fold each ear in half and ladder stitch in place using Figure 2 as a guide to the correct placing. Work some bracing stitches between the ears and through the head to hold the ears erect.

Nostrils Glue a 2.5cm (1in) diameter circle of felt on either side of the head where indicated in Diagram 4.

Eyelashes These are optional. On a dark coloured horse it is more effective to leave the eyes without lashes so that the eyes show up more against the toy skin. A light coloured horse is improved with dark felt lashes. If using lashes, the top curved edge of each is stitched immediately above the eye, and the bottom edge of the felt piece is then cut to form the lashes and left free. If the felt is rather thin, then stiffen the lashes with clear all-purpose adhesive and shape the lashes into an upward curve before finally dry.

Harness Using Figure 2 and Diagram 4 as a guide, proceed as follows. At (a) on the diagram is the puppy collar secured round the horse as it would be placed around a puppy's neck. Remove from the holding end of each lead approximately 43.7cm (17in); this should leave a remainder of approximately 38.1cm (15in) on each lead.

Take one of these 43.7cm (17in) strips and glue it

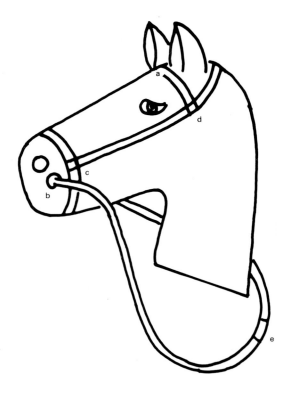

Diagram 4 Hobby horse bridle. a) Strap 1.3cm (½in) in front of the ears. b) Metal clips stitched to the mouth position 2.5cm (1in) down from the nose base. c-d) Distance between straps approx. 9cm (3½in). e) Glue cut ends together.

to the nose collar at (b) on both sides of the head, taking it from one side of the head, behind the ears, and down to (b) on the opposite side. Cut from the second 43.7cm (17in) strip a 20cm (8in) piece for the headband, and glue this across the forehead about 1.3cm (½in) in front of the ears at (c), on both sides of the head.

Bit Stitch a metal lead clip to either side of the mouth with each end matching to (b), leaving the metal pieces at the ends of the leads attached. Glue the previously cut ends of the leads together, overlapping the ends by 3.8cm (1½in), to form the reins.

3
KNITTED STRIPEY CAT AND KITTENS

SIZE
Cat – height 35.5cm (14in); Kittens – height 12.7cm (5in)

GRADING
Easy

TECHNIQUES
Stuffing and shaping a knitted toy. Creating a toy from a knitted strip

DESIGN BRIEF
A toy in knitted strip form to use oddments of knitting yarns and to demonstrate bulk filling in a knitted skin.

EVALUATION OF DESIGN BRIEF
The knitted strip principle is easy for both children and adults. Knitted strip toys are an excellent way of using up oddments of yarns. Try and choose yarns of comparable thickness and colour range: the toys will lose a degree of 'polish' if they are made in colours which do not tone or complement one another.

Tension is very important: if the knitter does not produce work which is even, this could result in the top filling showing through, and the toy would also become misshapen. If the knitting tension is rather loose, it may be necessary to make an inner bag from material to the size of the knitted strip, to hold the toy filling; the knitted strip is then applied over the bag as the toy skin.

MATERIALS REQUIRED
The cats illustrated were made using double knitting wool on size No. 10 knitting needles. Two 40g balls in orange were used, and one 40g ball in mink brown for the stripes. The mother cat strip measures 64.8cm (25½in) long. The kitten strips measure approximately 24.1cm (9½in) long. One metre (39in) of ribbon is needed for the mother cat's neck bow, and 0.5m (16½in) of ribbon for each kitten's neck bow.

Oddments of felt were used for the features.

Toy filling. This must be lightweight, for example nylon or terylene. On no account use cut up stockings or tights, foam chips or waste products, as these would produce a misshapen article.

Figure 3. Knitted stripey cat and kittens

CONSTRUCTION

Mother cat Cast on 50 stitches in the main body colour yarn. Work 6 rows in garter stitch then change to the colour being used for the stripes and work 4 rows in garter stitch. These 10 rows form one pattern. Continue until 15 patterns have been worked. At this stage the strip measures approximately 38.1cm (15in). Work 6 rows in garter stitch in the main colour. Change to stocking stitch and work 70 rows. Cast off.

Tail

Cast on 18 stitches and, in garter stitch, work 6 rows main colour and 4 rows contrast, as on the main body. Work 9 repeats of the pattern plus 6 rows of the main colour. Cast off.

MAKING UP

With the right sides facing and the stripes lining up around the body, fold the knitted strip in half, i.e. the striped pieces lined up and the plain body colour head piece in half, also lined up (see Diagram 5a). Using backstitch, join the seams together down either side, leaving the back of the cat open at the neck where the stocking stitch edge meets the folded stripe piece (b). Turn to the right side.

Backstitch across each top corner of the plain

stocking stitch to form the ears (c), pulling the stitching in slightly to gather and curve the ears. The size of the ears will vary slightly according to the yarn tension. Cut out a felt lining for each ear, slightly smaller all round than the ear size, and stitch into place using a neat running stitch.

Stuff the head and the body with toy filling, taking care to mould the cat into shape using Figure 3 as a guide. Because of the simplicity of this toy, it is essential to give it a smooth outline, and the filling must therefore be well teased apart so that no lumps can be seen or felt through the knitted toy skin. However firm the tension, it will still stretch to a degree, and the resulting shape could, in some cases, be very poor. To avoid this, apply the filling in small quantities and constantly hold the toy away from you to study the resulting shape. When satisfied with the cat shape achieved, ladder stitch the back opening to close. Run a gathering thread round the neck and pull up to shape. Add the ribbon bow around the neck, and tie to the front, side or back of the cat, whichever is preferred.

Features Choose felt oddments in colours to tone with the cat skin, and cut out the features. Stitch into place using Figure 3 as a guide to placing. Work the whiskers in yarn to tone.

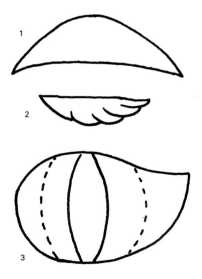

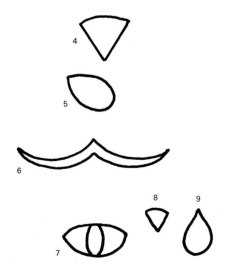

Full-size pattern pieces for cat and kitten features

Adult cat

1 Eyelids: cut two in fawn coloured felt.
2 Eyelashes: cut two in brown felt.
3 Eye base: cut two in fawn coloured felt. Inner circle

(indicated by broken line): cut two in yellow felt. Centre pupil: cut two in black felt.
4 Nose: cut one in pink felt.
5 Tongue: cut one in pink felt.
6 Mouth: cut one in fawn felt.

Kittens

7 Eye bases: cut four in orange felt. Pupil: cut four in brown felt.

8 Noses: cut two in light brown felt.

9 Tongues: cut two in orange felt.

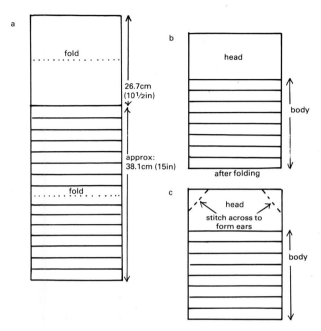

Knitted stripey cat. Body folding diagrams.
(not to scale)

Diagram 5   Body folding diagrams (not to scale)

Tail Fold the strip in half lengthways with the right sides facing, and stitch the seams together firmly leaving one end open to turn. Turn to the right side and stuff. Gather the open end and secure yarn. Ladder stitch the tail to the base of the cat at the centre back.

THE KITTENS

These are made in the same way as the mother cat, except in a reduced size. Cast on 14 stitches, working the pattern as for the large cat. Knit 6 pattern repeats plus 6 rows in garter stitch using the main colour. Change to stocking stitch and work 30 rows in the main colour. Cast off.

Kitten's tail Cast on 10 stitches and work 3 pattern repeats in garter stitch plus 6 rows in the main colour. Cast off.

4
OWL
FAMILY

Figure 4. Owl family

GRADING
Easy

DESIGN BRIEF
A basic outlined shaped toy

EVALUATION OF DESIGN BRIEF
Many birds and animals have been characterized into attractive soft toys, the owl possibly more than any other subject. This owl design developed one day at a craft class of disabled people where we were using a basic shape and each member was trimming that shape into a toy of their own design. Toys develop themselves and, with very little help from myself, my basic shape became the toy pattern given here. Children like families of toys, so, having designed father owl first, a little adjustment to the original pattern produced mother owl, followed by boy owl and baby owl. It was decided by the class that the owls should be depicted going on a picnic, so the basket containing a dead felt mouse was added.

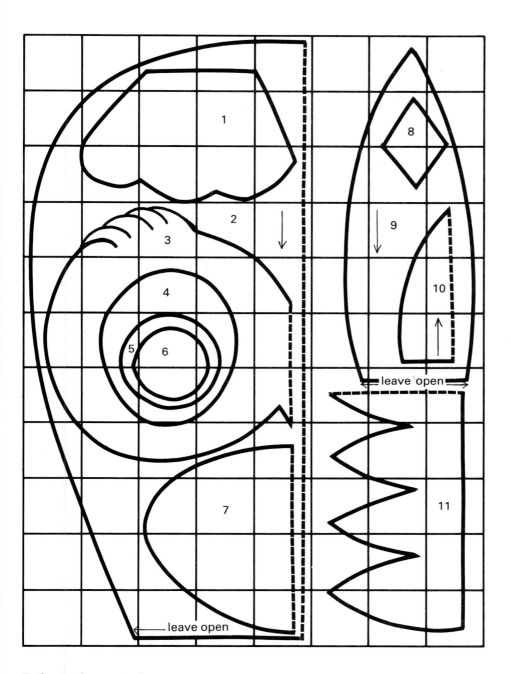

Father owl pattern pieces

1 Feet: cut four in orange felt.

2 Body: cut two in beige fur fabric (one reversed).

3 Face piece: cut one in felt to tone with the body fur fabric. Cut where indicated for the eyebrows.

4 Eyes: cut two in dark brown felt.

5 Eye bases: cut three in white felt (one piece to be cut in half for the eyelids).

6 Eye pupils: cut two in black felt.

7 Body base: cut one in fur fabric.

8 Beak: cut two in orange felt.

9 Wings: cut two in fur fabric, two in felt.

10 Ears: cut two in fur fabric, two in felt.

11 Feathers: cut in felt to length required, measured from one side body seam to the opposite side body seam.

CHOICE OF MATERIALS

Short pile fur fabric was used for the basic body shape. The felt feathers were stitched to the fabric backing and the fur pile then combed over the top edge of the felt feathers. Felt was used for all the feathers to provide a contrast in texture to the fur fabric.

FATHER OWL

SIZE
Height 28cm (11in)

MATERIALS REQUIRED
Beige coloured short pile fur fabric for body, ears and wings, 68.5cm (27in) × 30.5cm (12in)
Beige felt for eye base, 21.5cm (8½in) × 11.5cm (4½in)
Oddments of dark brown and white felt for the eye construction
Orange felt for feet and beak, 20.4cm (8in) × 20.4cm (8in)
Four strips of various brown and beige toned felts for the feathers, approximately 22.9cm (9in) × 5.7cm (2¼in) (in cutting the feather shapes from the felt strips, the cut oddments remaining can be used for the wing and brow feathers)
A piece of beige felt for the wing and ear linings, 17.8cm (7in) × 15.3cm (6in)
Two pipe-cleaners for wing stiffeners
A piece of strong card as lining for the owl base and feet

CONSTRUCTION
Cut out the pattern pieces as listed.

Body With right sides facing, pin the curved outside edge leaving the bottom straight edge open. Backstitch. Insert the base and stitch into position leaving one side open to stuff. Turn to the right side and stuff firmly without making the owl too rotund. Insert the card base cut a little smaller than the pattern base. Insert more filling prior to ladder stitching the opening in the base to close.

Body feathers Starting at the base with the darkest toned feathers, part the fur fabric pile in a line across the body and stitch the top straight edge of the felt feathers to the backing of the fur fabric using a neat running stitch. Comb the pile downwards over this sewn seam. Treat the other felt feather strips in the same way, slightly overlapping the feather points in between the previously applied strip. Continue in this way, applying all the feather strips working from the darkest toned felt up to the lightest coloured feathers.

To neaten the final strip, stitch approximately eight single feathers across the body. These single feathers are the oddments cut from the body feathers when shaping them in their original strip of felt. Insert a 2.5cm (1in) × 1.3cm (½in) piece of white felt cut into tiny feathers along one edge, under the beak placing, and stitch to hold.

Ears For each ear, place one fur fabric and one felt lining right sides together. Pin and then backstitch round the outside edge leaving the bottom straight edge open. Turn to the right side. Overstitch the bottom straight edge and pull up slightly; put a holding stitch, then apply to the body using ladder stitching. Figure 4 will aid the correct placing of the ears. The ears should have the felt lining facing the seams on the side of the body (see Diagram 6).

Diagram 6 Ear placing for owls

Eyes Stitch the eye base in position on the body as shown on the graph. Stitch on to this base the eye construction as shown, with the addition of the eyelids which are stitched to the top half of the eye piece No. 5 over the eye piece No. 6.

Beak Using Copydex or a similar latex-based adhesive, glue the two beak pieces together, leaving the top edge free from adesive and, when nearly dry, shape to form the beak. Stitch to the eye base over the centre front point.

Wings For each wing, place together one fur fabric piece and one felt lining with the right sides facing.

Pin then stitch around the outside curved edge leaving the bottom straight edge open. Turn to the right side. Insert a pipe-cleaner into one long edge and stitch to hold in place.

Close the opening and, using ladder stitch, apply a wing to each side seam on the body, the bottom of each wing to be approximately 5cm (2in) up the side of the body from the base, with the felt lining to the inside of the wings. Add three felt feathers to each wing from the wing tip for approximately 5cm (2in), the feathers to be facing towards the wing tip. Add some single felt feathers to the brow of the owl above the centre dip on the eye base.

Feet Place in pairs and overstitch the outside edge leaving the larger straight edge open. Insert a card lining cut a little smaller than the pattern, into each foot. Overstitch the straight edge to close. Ladder stitch to the body base at an angle (see Diagram 7). Stand the owl upright and ladder stitch along the top of each foot to the body base to secure.

owl's eye base pattern by approximately 1.3cm (½in) (see Diagram 8).

CONSTRUCTION

The construction of the mother owl is the same as for the father owl, with the exception that the eye base has no eyebrows cut into it, instead the eyelashes are inserted behind the top curve on the eyelids.

The colouring of the original mother owl was as follows:

Body	White fur fabric
Feathers	White felt
Eye base	Peach coloured felt
Eye construction	Light brown felt base, white eye base and eyelid, dark brown pupil
Beak	Yellow felt
Wing linings	White felt
Feet	Pale orange felt

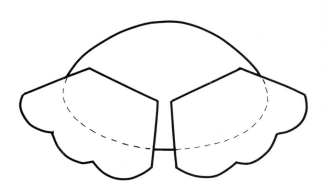

Diagram 7   Placing of feet on body base

MOTHER OWL

SIZE
Height 25.4cm (10in)

MATERIALS REQUIRED
All the pattern pieces and material requirements with the exception of the eye base and body are the same as for the father owl. The body height is 25.4cm (10in), the width 22.9cm (9in). The eye base is 17.8cm (7in) across by 8.3cm (3¼in) deep. Simply cut down the eye base circles on the father

Figure 5.   Mother owl

Diagram 8   Method of reduction from father owl pattern piece to size required for mother owl pattern

23

BOY OWL

Figure 6. Boy owl

SIZE
Height 11.5cm (4½in)

MATERIALS AND CONSTRUCTION
Constructed as the father owl, but omitting any body or wing feathers and the body base. The beak is glued to the eye base from the top to the bottom (see Figure 6 for placing). The eye construction is glued together and applied with a latex-based adhesive. The feet pieces are glued together in pairs then stitched to the body. The glue acts as a stiffener for the feet so they do not require card linings.

The jar to hold the fish is cut from a plastic container originally used as packaging for cocktail sticks. The small fish shapes are cut in thin coloured card and glued to the inside of the jar. Small narrow strips of green raffia are glued to the inside of the jar as weeds. Thin wire for the handle is inserted into a hole made with a thick sewing needle on either side of the top of the jar. If not considered safe for the recipient, substitute strong thread for the handle and stiffen with a little glue. The fishing net is made from a piece of fine terylene net 5cm (2in) × 5cm (2in) gathered along one edge, then glued together to form the fishing net. It is then secured to the top of a plastic drinking straw cut to a length of 11.5cm (4½in). Thin dowelling or strong weaving cane could be used.

The colouring of the original boy owl was as follows:

Body	Beige coloured fur fabric
Eye base	Cream coloured felt
Eye construction	Medium brown, white and black felt
Beak	Light orange felt
Feet	Bright orange felt

The boy owl can be made from oddments of materials. The largest amount required is the fur fabric for the body and wings – a piece 30.5cm (12in) × 22.9cm (9in).

BABY OWL

The construction is the same as for the boy owl. This baby owl has a body base which is inserted as the adult owls' bases. The wings have no felt linings as they are folded in half and stitched lengthways prior to being applied to the body. The feet on the baby owl are in yellow felt.

OWL PICNIC BASKET

MATERIALS REQUIRED

The mouse Grey felt 13.4cm (5¼in) × 9cm (3½in)
Oddments of pink felt for the ear linings
A hank of Turabast (coloured synthetic raffia), or natural raffia
A piece of small patterned cotton material 11.5cm (4½in) × 11.5cm (4½in)
A piece of weaving cane or covered wire 19.2cm (7½in) long

Figure 7. Picnic basket mouse

24

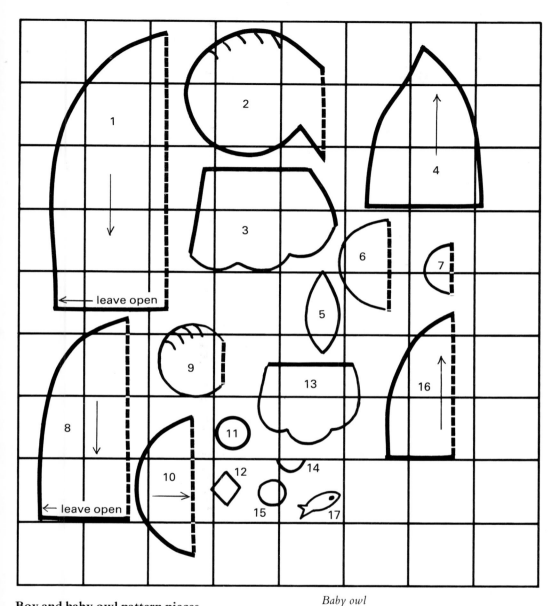

Boy and baby owl pattern pieces

Boy owl

1 Body: cut two in beige fur fabric (one reversed).
2 Eye piece: cut one in felt to tone with the body. Cut where indicated for eyebrows.
3 Feet: cut four in orange felt.
4 Wings: cut two in main body colour fur fabric. Cut two in felt to match for linings.
5 Beak: cut one in orange felt.
6 Eye bases: cut two in medium brown felt.
7 Eye whites: cut three in white felt (one is cut in half for the eyelids).

Baby owl

8 Body: cut two in beige fur fabric (one reversed).
9 Eye piece: cut one in felt to tone with the body. Cut where indicated for the eyebrows.
10 Body base: cut one in fur fabric to match body.
11 Eyes: cut two in beige felt.
12 Beak: cut one in orange felt.
13 Feet: cut two in yellow felt.
14 Eyes: cut two in brown felt.
15 Pupils: cut two in white felt.
16 Wings: cut two in main colour fur fabric; fold each wing in half.
17 Fish: cut two in felt.

CONSTRUCTION

Cut out all the pattern pieces as listed.

The mouse body Fold the body piece in half and backstitch the curved back edges of the body together, leaving the bottom straight edge open. Turn to the other side. Stuff firmly.

Cut a circle in grey felt to the size of the body base, and overstitch in place. Stitch the tail to the base of the back seam. Gather a small circle of black felt for the nose and stitch to the top point of the body. Embroider the shut eyes using black cotton. Add black cotton whiskers on either side of the nose.

Ears Glue a pink lining to each ear piece; whilst still damp, fold each ear in at the base to the centre. When dry, stitch to the body where indicated.

Paws and feet Overstitch, where indicated on the pattern, side by side with the paws facing the nose on the body. Place the feet in the same way a little lower on the body, where indicated.

Basket Make up, using the plaiting and stitching method, coiling to a basket of base size 7.6cm (3in) × 6.4cm (2½in) × 4.5cm (1¾in) deep, with a diameter top of 7.6cm (3in). The handle is a piece of weaving cane or covered wire measuring 19.2cm (7½in) with the raffia worked over it in blanket stitch.

Tablecloth Hem all round the 11.5cm (4½in) × 11.5cm (4½in) piece of patterned material. Place the mouse in the basket and cover with the tablecloth.

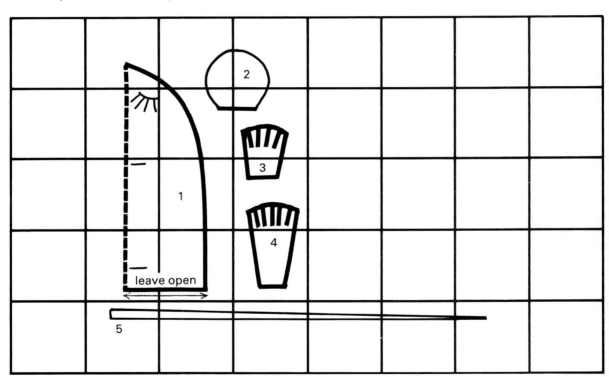

Mouse pattern pieces

1 Body: cut one in grey felt.
2 Ears: cut two in grey felt. Cut two in pink felt for linings.
3 Paws: cut two in grey felt. Cut where indicated.
4 Feet: cut two in grey felt. Cut where indicated.
5 Tail: cut one in grey felt.

5
FUR
CIRCLE
LION

advisable to have the head, feet and tail made from one type and colour of fur fabric, as this will form the toy into a positive subject; too many variations in colour tone can appear rather disjointed.

Acrylic long pile shaggy fur fabric 28cm (11in) × 35.5cm (14in) for the mane and tail tip, in light beige or blonde colour

Oddments of yellow and orange felt for the eyes

Scraps of pink felt for the mouth and pad markings

Toy filling for the head and feet

Rolled elastic 5.75m (6¼ yd)

Six 2.5cm (1in) diameter buttons

Horsehair for the whiskers

CONSTRUCTION

Cut out the pattern pieces and circles as listed. The fur fabric circles must be cut out separately, which is rather time consuming. The elastic quantities may require adjusting due to the possible variation in bulk of the pile on the fur fabric being used by the reader.

The lion is constructed as the material circle tiger, using Diagram 11 for the order of threading the circles. Prepare the neck circles, one 17.8cm (7in) diameter of short pile fur fabric, and one 17.8cm (7in) diameter circle of shaggy pile fur fabric; these must be cut in half.

Figure 8. Fur circle lion

SIZE
Reclining, measured from tip of the tail to the tip of the outstretched front legs – 99cm (39in)

GRADING
Moderately difficult

TECHNIQUES
The use of fur fabric circles to produce a cuddly toy

MATERIALS REQUIRED
1.25m (49in) of 1.22m (48in) wide beige short pile fur fabric. Oddments of toning fur fabric can be used provided the bulk of each fabric is similar. It is

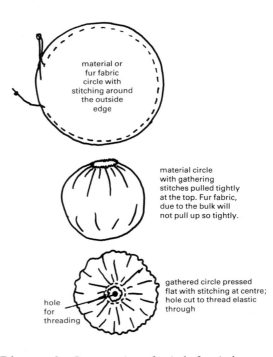

material or fur fabric circle with stitching around the outside edge

material circle with gathering stitches pulled tightly at the top. Fur fabric, due to the bulk will not pull up so tightly.

hole for threading

gathered circle pressed flat with stitching at centre; hole cut to thread elastic through

Diagram 9   Construction of a circle for circle toys

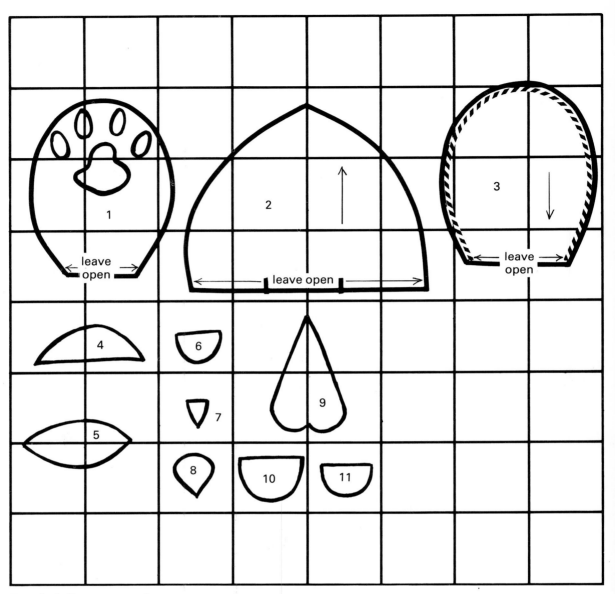

Fur circle lion pattern pieces

Head: Two 15.3cm (6in) diam. circles in short pile light beige fur fabric

Neck: One 17.8cm (7in) diam. circle short pile fur fabric
One 17.8cm (7in) diam. circle shaggy pile fur fabric

Body: Two 17.8cm (7in) diam. circles short pile fur fabric
Ten 20.4cm (8in) diam. circles short pile fur fabric
One 16cm (6¼in) diam. circle short pile fur fabric
One 14cm (5½in) diam. circle short pile fur fabric
One 12.1cm (4¾in) diam. circle short pile fur fabric
One 10.3cm (4in) diam. circle short pile fur fabric
One 7.6cm (3in) diam. circle short pile fur fabric

Legs: Four legs each consisting of one 10.3cm (4in) diam. circle, 20 7.6cm (3in) diam. circles and one 7cm (2¾in) diam. circle

1 Foot pads: cut four in dark beige felt.
Paw markings: cut a set for each foot in pale pink felt.

2 Ears: cut four in light beige fur fabric.

3 Feet: cut four in light beige fur fabric.

4 Eyelids: cut two in dark beige felt.

5 Eye bases: cut two in orange felt.

6 Eye centres: cut two in yellow felt.

7 Eye pupils: cut two in black felt.

8 Nose: cut one in pale pink felt.

9 Nose base: cut one in felt to match the eyelids.

10 Mouth base: cut one in same colour felt as nose base.

11 Mouth: cut one in pale pink felt.

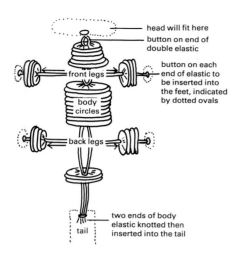

- head will fit here
- button on end of double elastic

front legs

button on each end of elastic to be inserted into the feet, indicated by dotted ovals

body circles

back legs

two ends of body elastic knotted then inserted into the tail

tail

Diagram 10   Construction for a four-legged subject

Join one shaggy half to one short pile fur fabric half on both of the circles. With the right sides facing, place these completed circles together, matching both shaggy halves and both plain halves. Stitch the circles together around the outside edge, leaving a 7.6cm (3in) opening at the top of the short pile fur fabric. Turn to the right side. Ladder stitch the opening to close.

Body Elastic measurement 76.2cm (30in) folded in half. Proceed as for the circle tiger, replacing the neck circles by the prepared half plain, half shaggy circle combination.

Legs Construct as for the tiger using 55.8cm (22in) single rolled elastic for the front legs and 60.9cm (24in) single elastic for the back legs.

Feet When placing the fur fabric top half of each foot on to the felt pads, first gather the outside edge of the curved fur fabric top foot piece, where indicated on the pattern, until it fits the foot pad, and secure the thread. With the right sides facing, pin the top and bottom of the foot together and stitch, leaving the straight edge open. Turn to the right side, stuff firmly and apply as for the tiger. Treat the other feet in the same way.

The ankle circles on the lion are stitched to the back edge of each foot, leaving the front of the feet protruding (see Diagram 12). Add the pad markings using neat running stitches. These markings can either be applied before constructing the feet or added afterwards.

Tail Cut a piece of the short pile fur fabric to measure 7.6cm (3in) × 29.2cm (11½in). Cut a piece of shaggy pile fur fabric 7.6cm (3in) × 7.6cm (3in). Stitch to the end of the tail, making sure that

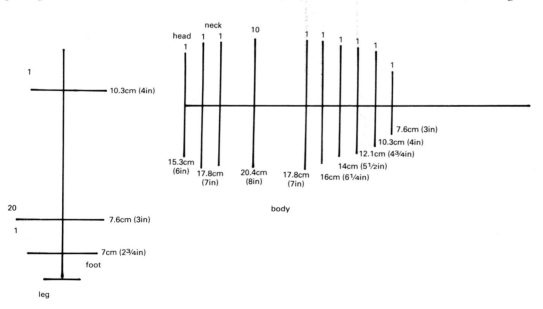

Diagram 11   Circle construction for leg and body (not to scale)

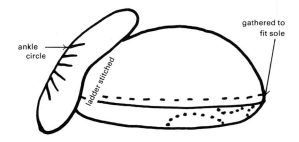

Diagram 12   Foot placing on ankle circle

the pile lines on both fabrics match up. With the right sides facing, fold the tail in half and backstitch the entire length together, leaving the top straight edge open. Turn to the right side and fold in half lengthways a second time and ladder stitch the edges together. This will reduce the tail width by half and at the same time form the tail stuffing. Apply the tail to the body elastic as for the tiger.

Head   With the right sides facing, stitch two 15.3cm (6in) diameter short pile fur fabric circles together around the outside edge, leaving a 5cm (2in) opening. Turn to the right side and stuff, shaping the circle well but avoiding filling it too tightly which would distort the shape. Ladder stitch the opening together to close.

Ears   Place the ear pieces together in pairs. With the right sides facing, backstitch around the outside edge, leaving the bottom straight edge open. Turn to the right side and work a holding stitch. Over-stitch the straight edge and pull gently to form a curve and fasten off. Treat both the ears in the same way. Pin into place on the head using Diagram 13 and Figure 8 as a guide to placing.

Pin the eyes, nose and mouth into place. By only pinning at this stage it is possible to rearrange the features until the required expression is achieved. Neatly stitch all the features in place. Cut two pieces of shaggy pile fur fabric 2.5cm (1in) × 0.7cm (¼in) and, with the pile line facing up the ears, ladder stitch one piece at the inside base of each ear where indicated.

Whiskers   Apply each side of the nose piece where indicated on the pattern graph.

Mane   Cut a piece of shaggy pile fur fabric to measure 35.5cm (14in) × 15.3cm (6in). Stitch round the head X–X following the seam line, with the pile line facing down the body. Comb the pile

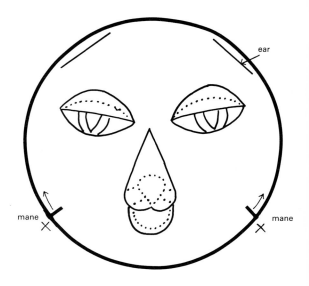

Diagram 13   Diagram of feature placing

on the mane to match the pile line of the neck circle. Combing downwards on the neck circle forms a long pile fur chest to the lion and completes the head shaping. Stitch the top curve on the short pile half of the neck circle to the back of the head circle at the centre of the head.

When the lion has been completed it is noticeable that, due to the bulk of the fur fabric circles, it is considerably larger than the tiger. This lion was designed as a cuddly toy and the fur fabric circles make it very nice to handle. Whilst in its present construction it is not suitable to string as a puppet, if longer lengths of elastic were used, resulting in looser stringing, this would produce the flexibility required for movement and the lion would make an excellent string puppet subject.

30

6
MATERIAL CIRCLE TIGER

SIZE
Reclining position from the tip of the tail to the tip of the outstretched front legs – 50.8cm (20in)

GRADING
Moderately difficult

MATERIALS REQUIRED
The circles for the body and legs of the tiger are made from oddments of lightweight dress materials in yellow and black. The circle sizes are given in the instructions.

Head, tail and feet A 45.7cm (18in) square of yellow felt

Foot pads, nose base and facial markings Black felt 21.5m (8½in) × 6cm (3in)

Ear linings, nose and tongue Pink felt 10.3cm (4in) × 10.3cm (4in)

Figure 9. Material circle tiger

31

Toy filling for the head, tail and feet
Black rolled elastic for the stringing, 111.8cm (44in)
Six 2cm (¾in) diameter buttons

Eyes Scraps of light and dark orange felt

Card to make the circle templates

CONSTRUCTION

Cut out all the pattern pieces as listed. To make the material circles, it is necessary first to cut in card the template circles in the following sizes: 8cm (3⅛in), 10.3cm (4in), 12.1cm (4¾in), 14cm (5½in), 16cm (6¼in), 17.8cm (7in), 20.2cm (7⅞in) in diameter. Make a hole in the centre of each circle and mark each template with its size.

Cutting out and marking It is not necessary to cut out each material circle separately; the number you will be able to cope with at one cutting will be determined by the thickness of the material. Mark the centres of the material circles through the hole pierced in each card template. If using a light coloured material, a pencil can be used for the marking; on dark coloured material use tailor's chalk.

Stitching Make a hole at the centre of a circle, then, using strong thread, gather, using small stitches, around the outside edge. Pull up the gathering tightly and fasten off at the centre. Flatten the circle with the palm of the hand. All the circles are made in the same way (see Diagram 9).

Body circles Make circles for the body starting at the tail end with one black 8cm (3⅛in) diameter circle, one yellow 10.3cm (4in) diameter, one black 12.1cm (4¾in) diameter, one yellow 12.7cm (5in) diameter, one black 16cm (6¼in) diameter, one yellow 17.8cm (7in) diameter, ten 20.2cm (7⅞in) diameter black and yellow alternating, one black 17.8cm (7in) diameter, and four 17.8cm (7in) diameter yellow and black alternating.

Stringing Before commencing stringing the toy, it is useful to be aware of the possible variations in material weights which will alter the required lengths of elastic. There may well be a difference in the weight of the material used by the reader and those used by the author for the illustrated tiger. As a general guide, when stringing the circles onto the elastic, pull the elastic until the circles are held firmly, but not too tightly together. If they are strung too tightly, the circle toy will not be flexible; if too loose, the elastic will show and the tiger will lose body shaping. If using thicker material, then allow longer lengths of elastic when threading; if the toy then becomes correspondingly larger it may be necessary to enlarge the head, feet and tail.

Body assembly Take a 45.7cm (18in) length of rolled elastic and fold it in half. Thread a button securely on one end and place it at the centre of the folded elastic. Thread the circle on the open ends of the elastic, starting at the tail end and following the order given in the making of the body circles. Knot the elastic and add a button firmly to the end.

Front legs Make 42 8cm (3⅛in) diameter circles alternating black and yellow. Knot one end of a piece of the rolled elastic cut to measure 30.5cm (12in). Thread 21 of the 8cm (3⅛in) diameter circles on to the elastic, starting with a black circle and alternating black and yellow. Place the end of the elastic through the double body elastic between the fifth and sixth circle counted from the neck end. Thread on the remaining 21 8cm (3⅛in) diameter circles ending with a black circle. Knot the elastic.

Back legs Each back leg requires 21 8cm (3⅛in) diameter circles, two 10.3cm (4in) diameter circles and one 12.1cm (4¾in) diameter circle. String in this size order on to a length of elastic measuring 35.5cm (14in) starting with a black circle and alternating black with yellow circles. Then apply through the body as for the front legs, inserting the elastic through the body between circles seven and eight counted from the tail end.

Feet Place the yellow felt pattern pieces together in pairs and stab stitch together, leaving open where indicated, and also the bottom straight edge open. Insert a black felt pad into the base of each foot and stab stitch in place. Stuff each foot firmly using lightweight toy filling. Add a button on to the end of each leg elastic and insert into each foot. Stuff firmly around each button and close the top opening on each foot.

Taking the circle immediately above each foot, stitch the circle firmly to the top of the foot. This adds strength and is a double safety measure against the button being pulled out. Treat each foot in the same way.

Tail Cut a piece of yellow felt to measure 21.5cm

Tiger pattern pieces

1 Head: cut two in yellow felt.
2 Mouthpiece: cut one in black felt.
3 Mouth lining: cut one in pink felt.
4 Ear pieces: cut two in black felt. Solid line below dotted ear placing line indicates placing of ear pieces.
5 Feet: cut eight in yellow felt.
6 Foor pads: cut four in black felt.
7 Eye pupils: cut two in black felt.

8 Eyelids: cut two in black felt.
9 Eye centres: cut two in bright orange felt.
10 Eye bases: cut two in pale orange felt.
11 Nose: cut one in pale pink felt.
12 Nose base: cut one in black felt.
13 Tail stripes: cut eight in black felt.
14 Ears: cut two in yellow felt. Cut two pink felt linings. Dotted line on head indicates correct placing.
15 Facial stripes: cut seven in black felt.

(8½in) × 7.6cm (3in). Fold in half and backstitch together. Taper to a point about 5cm (2in) from the tail end; the surplus felt will then form a filling for the end of the tail when it is turned inside out. Turn the tail inside out and stuff lightly. Turn a 0.7cm (¼in) hem at the top straight edge and gather over the button at the tail end of the body; stitch the smallest circle at the end of the body to the tail. Add narrow black felt stripes around the tail, spacing them at approximately 2.5cm (1in) intervals.

Head In yellow felt cut two 14cm (5½in) diameter circles. Place together and backstitch around the outside edge, leaving an opening to enable turning. Turn inside out. Stuff firmly and close the opening. When stuffing the head avoid it becoming too rotund; keep it fairly flat to continue the flat circle image.

Ears Place one yellow ear piece and one pink felt lining together. Stab stitch around the outside edge, leaving the bottom straight edge open. Overstitch along the bottom straight edges and pull up slightly to form a curve. Ladder stitch to the head where indicated. Treat the other ear in the same way. Stitch a black felt ear piece along the base at the front of each ear.

Eyes To produce a gleaming appearance to the eyes use pale orange felt for each eye base, a brighter orange for the eyes, and black felt for the pupils and eyelids.

Nose Stitch a pink felt tongue and nose to the black felt nose and mouth base where indicated on the pattern. Neatly stitch all the features on to the face, also adding the facial stripes.

Applying the head to the body Make a small slit in the back of the head circle 5cm (2in) up from the neck at the centre. Insert the button at the neck end of the body elastic into the slit at the back of the head. Insert more toy filling at this stage to pad all around the button, especially at the back. Close the slit firmly with overstitching.

Attach the first neck circle to the head by stitching around the circle approximately 3.8cm (1½in) from the centre hole; this will leave the outside edge of the circle free to stand out around the base of the head.

If there is any doubt in the toymaker's mind about the desirability of using buttons in the construction of this toy, then omit the buttons and use the following method. To replace each button, gather a small circle and fill with a heavy quality toy filling; gather to form a ball, and attach to a knot at the end of each elastic. This stuffed ball can then be inserted into whatever part is being added, for example head and feet, and stitched as per the button method.

7
FUR CIRCLE RABBIT

SIZE
Height 58.4cm (23in)

GRADING
Easy

TECHNIQUES
Stringing a fur circle toy. Use of the Suffolk Puff patchwork principles to create a toy requiring very little stuffing

DESIGN BRIEF
An inexpensive easy-to-make soft toy with good play value

CHOICE OF MATERIALS
Circle toys are an excellent way of using oddments of materials. Due to the bulk of a gathered fur circle, a toy in this medium requires less material than, for example, a toy made from lightweight dress materials. To produce a well-balanced toy, it is necessary to use materials of equal weight and to avoid mixing fabrics, as this could result in a poorly shaped toy.

If purchasing material for a particular toy project, beware that quantities can sometimes be very misleading; for example, 17.8cm (7in) diameter circles can soon use up 1m (39in) of material. Fur fabric circles may appear an expensive way of making a toy, but very little toy filling is required, and the fur fabric circles produce a very cuddly soft toy.

MATERIALS REQUIRED
This toy was designed to use oddments of fur fabric. The original rabbit was made in red, green, orange and white fur fabric, using fabric which had been left over from various other toymaking projects. The colours have been listed to differentiate between the shirt and the trouser circles. Should you wish to make the toy in special colours of your choice, it is an easy task to work out the material quantities required by dividing the circle diameters into the width and depth of the material and purchasing the correct quantity to the nearest measurement.

Head, hands, tail and feet White short pile fur fabric 36.8cm (14½in) × 36.8cm (14½in)

Ear linings Pink felt 6.4cm (2½in) × 13.4cm (5¼in)

Figure 10. Fur circle rabbit

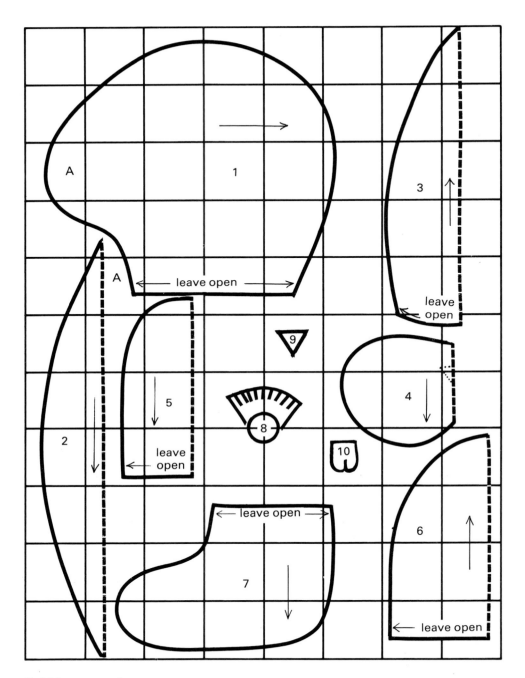

Rabbit pattern pieces

1 Head: cut two in fur fabric (one reversed).
2 Head gusset: cut one in fur fabric.
3 Ears: cut two in fur fabric. Cut two in felt for the ear linings.
4 Muzzle: cut one in fur fabric.
5 Paws: cut four in fur fabric (two reversed).

6 Tail: cut two in fur fabric (one reversed).
7 Feet: cut four in fur fabric (one reversed).
8 Eye backs: cut two in black felt. Cut where indicated to form the eyelashes.
9 Nose: cut one in pink felt.
10 Teeth: cut one in card and two in white felt.

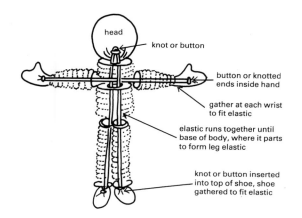

head

knot or button

button or knotted
ends inside hand

gather at each wrist
to fit elastic

elastic runs together until
base of body, where it parts
to form leg elastic

knot or button inserted
into top of shoe, shoe
gathered to fit elastic

Diagram 14   An upright figure construction for circle toys

Eye backs and lashes Oddments of black felt

Nose Oddment of pink felt

Teeth Small piece of white felt and card for stiffening

Toy filling A small quantity for stuffing the head, hands and feet

Horsehair for the whiskers
Strong cord for the stringing, 121.9cm (48in)
Six buttons approximately 2.5cm (1in) in diameter; raincoat buttons with a metal shank are ideal

CONSTRUCTION

Cut out all the pattern pieces as listed. Make circle card templates for the fur circles to the following measurements: 12.7cm (5in) diameter, 15.3cm (6in) diameter, 17.8cm (7in) diameter and 20.4cm (8in) diameter. Make a hole in the centre of each one so that the centre of each fur circle can be marked.

FUR CIRCLES REQUIRED

Collar Cut one 17.8cm (7in) diameter circle in orange fur fabric.

Shirt (body) Cut three 20.4cm (8in) diameter circles in red fur fabric.

Shirt sleeves (arms) Cut ten 15.3cm (6in) diameter circles in red fur fabric, i.e. five circles for each arm.

Wrists Cut two 12.7cm (5in) diameter circles in red fur fabric, one for each sleeve.

Trousers (body) Cut four 20.4cm (8in) diameter circles in green fur fabric.

Trousers (legs) Cut 16 17.8cm (7in) diameter circles in green fur fabric, eight for each leg.

Socks Cut two 12.7cm (5in) diameter circles in red fur fabric, one for each leg.

CIRCLE CONSTRUCTION

Using a strong thread, gather around each circle with small running stitches on the fur pile side of the fabric. Pull up tightly and fasten off. Press with a hand to flatten, and then make a hole in the centre of each circle so that they can be threaded onto the cord.

THREADING THE CIRCLES

The body Fold a length of cord measuring 81.3cm (32in) in half and attach a button securely to the centre fold of this body cord. Thread on the 17.8cm (7in) collar circle. Lay to one side.

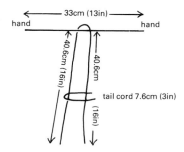

33cm (13in)

hand   hand

40.6cm (16in)

40.6cm (16in)

tail cord 7.6cm (3in)

(16in)

Diagram 15   Cord sizes. Total measurement of body cord: 81.3cm (32in); total measurement of cord: 81.3cm (32in) + 33cm (13in) + 7.6cm (3in) = 121.9cm (48in)

Arms Cut a piece of strong cord to measure 33cm (13in). Secure a button to one end of the cord, and thread on a 12.7cm (5in) wrist circle, with the gathering at the centre of the circle facing away from the button. Thread on five 15.3cm (6in) shirt sleeve circles, with the gathering direction alternating so that the smooth sides match together, and also the gathered sides.
    Thread the end of the arm cord through the folded body cord below the collar circle, and thread on the remaining five arm circles, finishing with a

wrist circle. Tie a button to the end of the cord, but at this stage do not secure firmly. Using the body cord still doubled, thread this through the three red 20.4cm (8in) shirt body circles, followed by three green 20.4cm (8in) trouser body circles. Lay to one side.

Tail With the right sides facing, place the tail pieces together; pin then backstitch together, leaving the bottom straight edge open. Turn to the right side. Stuff firmly and gather the bottom edge – do not pull up.

Cut a piece of strong cord to measure 7.6cm (3in); fold in half around the two body cords under the three trouser body circles, and attach a button to the tail cord ends. Insert this into the stuffed tail, add more filling around the button and pull up the tail gathering tightly. Stitch this firmly to the folded double tail cord.

Thread both the body cords through the fourth 20.4cm (8in) trouser body circle. Divide the body cords for the legs, and thread eight of the 17.8cm (7in) trouser leg circles on to each cord, ending at the ankles with a 12.7cm (5in) sock circle. Temporarily tie a button to each cord end.

Fabrics will vary in thickness, so an adjustment to the cord lengths on your circle rabbit may be required. It is at this stage that any alterations in the cords should be made. As a general guide, the circles should be firm without being squashed on the cords, with no gaps between the circles showing. If necessary, to obtain the firmness required, cut off any surplus cord length on the arms and legs and secure the buttons firmly to the cord ends, prior to applying the head, paws and feet.

Feet With the right sides facing, place together in pairs. Pin then backstitch around the outside edges, leaving the top straight edges open. Turn to the right side and stuff.

Gather the open straight edge on each foot and pull up to close, inserting a button on the end of a leg cord into each one. Before closing, stuff firmly around each button, then pull up the gathering tightly and fasten off firmly to the cords. Ladder stitch the sock circle on each leg to the top of each foot; this will add extra strength.

Paws With the right sides facing, place the paw pieces together in pairs; pin then backstitch together leaving the straight edges open. Turn to the right side and stuff.

Run a gathering thread around the open edge on each paw and, before closing, insert the button on each arm end and into a paw, adding more toy filling prior to closing. Fasten off firmly, also stitching to the arm cords. Ladder stitch a wrist circle to each paw to add extra strength.

Head With the right sides facing, place the two side head pieces together and pin, then backstitch from the front base of the neck to (a). Insert the head gusset, matching (a) on the gusset to (a) on the head pieces. Pin then backstitch first one side of the gusset from the nose to the back of the head, then fasten off the thread. Stitch the other side of the gusset in the same way. Turn to the right side.

Insert the safety lock eyes, first through the felt eye backs and then through the fur fabric.

Stuff the head firmly, and gather the bottom neck edge and pull up. Before finally closing, insert the button attached to the top of the body cord into the head, adding more toy filling. Pull the gathers up tightly and fasten off. Ladder stitch the 17.8cm (7in) collar circle to the neck.

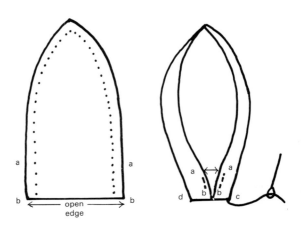

Diagram 16 Rabbit ear construction. Fold the outside edges to the centre of the ear matching (a–a) and (b–b). Ladder stitch the edges of the ear together from (a) to (b). Place a holding stitch but do not detach the thread; take the needle and thread out at corner (c), and place another holding stitch with the ear erect. Ladder stitch the ear to the head across the ear base to (d), then ladder stitch behind the ear to the head across to (c). Fasten off.

Ears (Diagram 16) With fabrics facing, place the ear pieces together in pairs, one fur fabric and one felt lining. Pin then stitch around the outside edges, leaving the bottom straight edges open. Turn to the right side. Fold the bottom corners on each ear until they meet at the centre of the ear base. Stitch to hold the fold. Do this for both ears, and ladder stitch to the head.

Provided the head was well stuffed, the ears should stand erect, but it may be necessary to add bracing stitches (Diagram 17a) from the inside base of one ear, through the head to the inside base of the

Whiskers Insert strands of horsehair either side of the muzzle approximately 2.5cm (1in) from the embroidered mouth division.

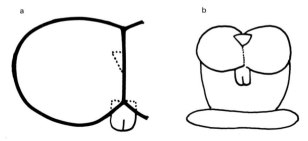

Diagram 18 a) Nose and teeth placing on the muzzle piece. b) Neck circle stitched to the neck base of the head.

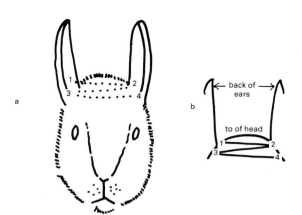

Diagram 17 Bracing stitches: this is a useful method, used sparingly, but the stitches will not compensate for bad designing or inadequate stuffing. a) Ears attached on either side of the rabbit's head; dotted lines show bracing stitches. b) Section showing solid line of actual stitching

opposite ear. Go back through the head and place stitches just below the previous ones, then pull on the thread until the ears are upright; fasten off.

Teeth and muzzle Cover the card with white felt, overstitching around the outside edge. Ladder stitch the top edge to the head, 5.7cm (2¼in) up the front seam measured from the neck circle. Ladder stitch the muzzle in place with the centre of the muzzle placed over the top of the teeth. Before finally closing, add toy filling inside the muzzle for shaping.

Nose Stitch the felt nose into place where indicated on the graph pattern, then, using three strands of embroidery stranded silk, add the mouth shaping as shown on the pattern.

8
EMBROIDERED MOUSE

SIZE
Height 25.4cm (10in)

GRADING
Easy

TECHNIQUES
Basic embroidery in toymaking

DESIGN BRIEF
A basic toy to use embroidery techniques as decoration

EVALUATION OF DESIGN BRIEF
If a toy is to have any embellishments, for example, embroidery, it is often more effective if the design is kept to a basic outline shape, permitting the embroidery to add the visual interest. Lightweight carpet wool was used for the embroidery on this mouse, and the colouring was extended to a plaited tail. It is not necessary to use intricate embroidery on a toy that is to be played with – a few simple stitches are sometimes all that is required.

The secret to a successful toy made in this way, is to have toning colouring with a strong connection between any additions; for example, in the case of the mouse pattern given here, the body and the tail follow through from pale orange to darker orange tones, to light browns and finally to dark brown.

Avoid being over fussy with any decorations, and have the decorating as a main feature. If this mouse was embroidered all down the front gusset as well as down the back, then one would detract from the other. An exception to this rule is if you require to produce texturing all over the toy skin. In this case, the stitches should be all the same style with the only variation being in their size. Feathering on a felt bird subject can be produced very effectively in this manner.

MATERIALS REQUIRED

Felt A piece of felt measuring 59.7cm (23½in) × 26.7cm (10½in)
Two contrasting ear linings in felt measuring 21.7cm (8½in) × 11.5cm (4½in)
Oddments of felt for the nose and eye construction

Thrums carpet wools or similar for the embroidery and the plaited tail, or leftover oddments of wool from knitting projects
Toy filling
Piece of smooth strong card cut a little smaller than the mouse base pattern

Figure 11.   Embroidered mouse

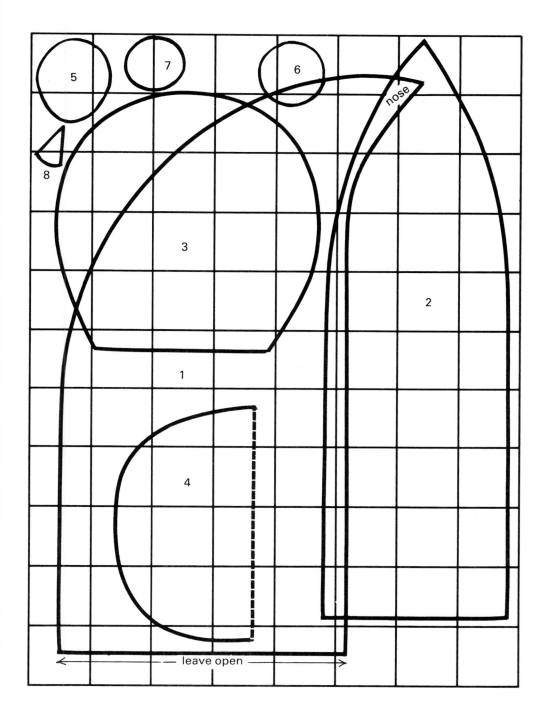

Mouse pattern pieces

1 Body: cut two in felt.

2 Front body gusset: cut one in felt.

3 Ears: cut two in main body colour felt and two contrasting felt linings.

4 Base: cut one in felt and one slightly smaller in strong smooth card.

5–8 Eye construction: cut two in felt for each pattern piece, the colours to graduate from light to dark (see Diagram 19).

CONSTRUCTION

Cut out the pattern pieces as listed.

Body Place the two body pieces together; pin then machine or hand backstitch from the top nose point down the curved back outside edge to the base. Insert the front body gusset, matching the top point on the gusset to the nose point on the body. Pin then backstitch the outside edge together, leaving the base open. Turn to the right side and stuff firmly, making sure that the toy skin retains a smooth surface.

Tail The tail is plaited carpet wool in a variety of toning shades complementary to the body and eye colouring. It starts 2.5cm (1in) wide at the body, tapering to 0.7cm (¼in) at the tail tip, which is tightly bound with the wool and stitched at the end to hold. A narrow toning terylene ribbon bow is added to the tail just behind the bound tip. After making the tail, put it to one side and proceed with the base.

Base Using latex-based adhesive, glue the card base lining on to the felt base, leaving the edge around the felt base free from the adhesive. Stab stitch this stiffened base into the base of the body, leaving an opening for the tail at the back. Just prior to closing, it may be necessary to add more filling then insert the tail into the base of the centre back seam and close.

Nose The nose is a 3.3cm (1¼in) diameter circle, gathered around the outside edge, then stuffed. The stitches are pulled up to form a ball which is then ladder stitched to the nose tip on the body.

Eyes Each eye comprises four pattern pieces graduating in colour tones to match the body, starting with the darker colour for the pupil and graduating to the lightest colour for the largest eye piece. It can add conformity to the toy if the ear linings are the same colour as the lightest eye piece. Stitch the eye pieces together, then glue to the body with a latex-based adhesive (i.e. Copydex).

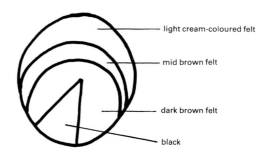

Diagram 19   Eye construction

Ears Place one ear piece and one lining together. Backstitch around the outside edge leaving the bottom straight edge open. Turn to the right side. Repeat for other ear. Fold each ear in half and stitch to the body using Figure 11 as a guide to placing.

BODY DECORATION

Whichever stitches are used, the embroidery on the toy needs to follow the back seam. The mouse illustrated had stitching which branched out from a central stem, with the addition of French knots scattered in between the branches. At the base of the back, French knots are surrounded by lazy daisy stitches. The embroidery extends from the base of the back to the top of the head just in front of the ears. See Diagram 62 for suggested suitable stitches to use.

9
PRAM COVER AND HANGING TOYS

GRADING
Moderately difficult

TECHNIQUES
Appliqué using the trapunto method

DESIGN BRIEF
A pair of soft toys suitable for hanging on a baby's pram

DEVELOPMENT OF DESIGN
To add a more interesting dimension to the pram toys, they were designed as a pair, with the theme of a boy rabbit giving a flower to a girl rabbit, and the extension of a matching pram cover echoing the design of the hanging toys. This is a useful concept, as many toy subjects are suitable to use in this medium. The appliqué motives are simply half of the body profile, sometimes requiring a slight alteration to the shape, with the addition of eyes, ears and tail where applicable. It is also very useful to be able to match the materials used to the colouring of the pram.

MATERIALS REQUIRED
Each baby rabbit, including the appliqué shape, requires 23.4cm (9¼in) × 30.5cm (12in) of short pile fur fabric; pink and blue were used for the original models.

Ear linings White fur fabric 17.8cm (7in) × 7.6cm (3in) is sufficient for one rabbit plus the appliqué shape and the half white circle on both tails

1m (39in) of pink baby ribbon for the girl rabbit
35.5cm (14in) of blue baby ribbon for the boy rabbit
Two small pieces of pink felt for the eyelids
Scraps of black felt for the eyelashes
Two pairs of blue 10mm safety lock eyes (only three eyes are used)
Scraps of green, white and yellow felt for the daisies
Black stranded embroidery silk for the mouth and nose markings, and for the French knots in the centre of the daisies
Toy filling

Pram cover Two pieces of short pile fur fabric 60.9cm (24in) × 81.3cm (32in). The pieces are given as a separate measurement to enable the reader to make the best use of the material width available. The cover can also be made with the two sides in different colours, if preferred.

CONSTRUCTION
Cut out all the pattern pieces as listed.

Rabbits Make two rabbits, one in pink fur fabric and one in blue, using the rabbit glove puppet baby rabbit pattern and instructions.

The girl rabbit has her eyes applied as per the instructions for the nightdress-case rabbits. Add a piece of the pink baby ribbon around the girl rabbit's neck, and tie in a small bow. Cut a 33cm (13in) length of the pink ribbon; fold in half and stitch to the top of the head between the ears. Fasten off. Tie a small pink ribbon bow and stitch in front of the hanging ribbon between the ears.

Cut a 33cm (13in) length of the blue ribbon, fold in half, turn in the ends of the ribbon neatly and stitch between the ears of the boy rabbit; he does not have a bow.

Daisy (Make two) Stitch the six petals together at a central point and fasten off. Gather the yellow centre, pull up and add some filling to form a small ball; put a holding stitch, then stitch to the centre of the white petals. Using two strands of the stranded embroidery silk, work French knots over the yellow centre.

Fold the stem in half lengthways and neatly overstitch the edges together; stitch to the centre of the daisy back. Stitch the back behind the white

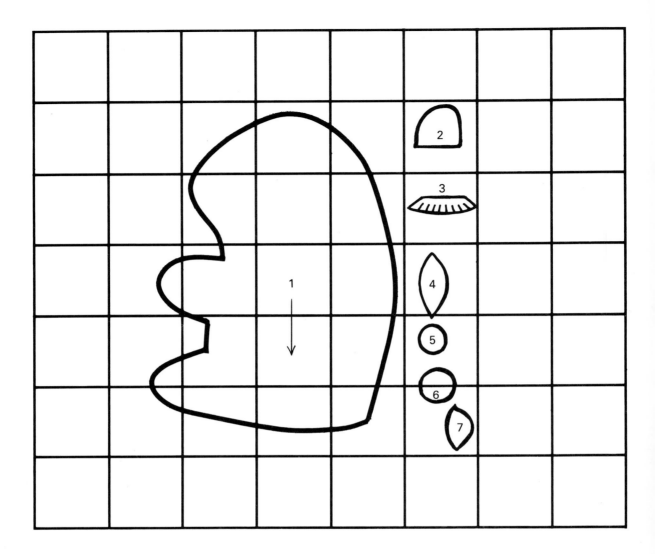

Appliqué shapes pattern pieces

1 Body: boy rabbit: cut one in blue short pile fur fabric; girl rabbit: cut one, reversed, in pink short pile fur fabric.
2 Eye: girl rabbit: cut one in pink felt.
3 Eyelashes: girl rabbit: cut one in black felt and cut where indicated.
4 Daisy petals: cut six in white felt for each daisy.
5 Daisy centre: cut one in yellow felt for each daisy.
6 Daisy back: cut one in green felt for each daisy.
7 Leaf: cut two in green felt for each daisy.

The stem of each flower is a piece of green felt measuring 1.3cm (½in) × 5cm (2in).

The ears for each appliquéd rabbit shape are made using the ear pattern for the rabbit glove puppet baby.

petals at the centre to cover the petal stitching. Add a leaf on either side of the stem towards the top, just under the flower. Stitch the flower to the right hand of the boy rabbit. The second flower will be used on the appliqué boy rabbit.

Appliqué rabbit shapes Insert a safety lock eye into the boy rabbit shape, and appliqué an eyelid and lashes on to the girl rabbit shape. With the pile line on the rabbit bodies lining up with the pile line on the pram cover, pin the rabbit shapes in place with the wrong side of the rabbit shapes placed on the right side of the cover fabric, approximately 33cm (13in) from the bottom edge of the cover and 22.9cm (9in) in from either side of the cover, the measurement being taken from each side edge to each rabbit back. There is a space between the rabbits' feet of 2cm (¾in).

Ladder stitch around the outside edge of each rabbit body to the pram cover fabric, making sure the cover is at all times laid flat, because otherwise on completion it could well have wrinkles around the appliquéd shapes.

Turn the cover over to the wrong side and make a small slit in the cover at the back of each appliquéd shape. Insert some toy filling into each rabbit through the slits, making sure that it is evenly placed without too much depth which would distort the cover. Close the slits using ladder stitching, taking care not to pull up too tightly. Turn the cover to the right side.

Ladder stitch the prepared extra ears on to the respective rabbits. Ladder stitch the tails in place. Add a neck ribbon and bow to the girl rabbit and stitch either side of the neck to hold. Stitch the extra flower to the boy rabbit's paw.

Pram cover Place the two 60.9cm (24in) × 81.3cm (32in) pieces of fur fabric with the right sides together, making sure that the pile lines on both pieces match. Pin then backstitch the outside edges together, leaving the top edge open. Turn to the right side and ladder stitch the open ends together to close.

Using a teazle brush, and holding the cover on the top edge, brush the cover and appliquéd shapes thoroughly, so that the shapes blend in with the cover fabric. Brush the ears and tails separately.

10
RABBIT NIGHTDRESS/ PYJAMA CASE

In the original nightcase the rabbits were made in pink fur fabric with pink felt ear linings. The pyjamas were in pale blue striped flannelette, and the nightdress in a very small pink and blue patterned cotton material. The bed material was in a blue and white check cotton with a pink flower design on it. The ribbon bows trimming the mob cap and the nightdress were pale pink. The broderie anglaise trimming and material were white. Thus all the materials toned or related to one another, making the end product more appealing than if mixed colours had been used.

As with other toy designs in this book, these rabbits are an ideal way of using up materials which may have been left over from other projects. The clothes only use small quantities, as they are applied to the rabbits for effect only, so their construction is very basic. Broderie anglaise can be rather expensive, and, if you wish to cut down on the cost, use the broderie anglaise only for the pillow and the sheet turnback and substitute plain white cotton material for the rest of the lining.

GRADING
Moderately difficult

TECHNIQUES
Making a functional case with the addition of models

DESIGN BRIEF
A nightdress/pyjama case making use of toy models

EVALUATION OF DESIGN BRIEF
This was not an easy project, as the models could easily have interfered with the space required for the child's nightwear. To resolve this, only the top half of each adult rabbit pattern was designed. A young child could be frustrated that all the toys are not removable from the bed, and therefore the baby rabbit was made to full size. Should a problem still exist, it may be necessary to extend the body lengths on the adult figures, making them similar to a glove puppet; they could then be removable.

CHOICE OF MATERIALS
If possible, the colouring of materials chosen should match or tone with the bedroom of the recipient. Whatever colours are used, it is essential for the overall effect that the fur fabric, bedclothes, nightdress and pyjamas should all tone.

MATERIALS REQUIRED

Body, head and arms For each adult a piece of short pile fur fabric 55.9cm (22in) × 50.8cm (20in)

Ear linings A piece of felt 12.7cm (5in) × 22.9cm (9in)

Baby rabbit The baby rabbit is made as for the rabbit glove puppet's baby (p. 78). The material quantities are therefore the same.

Oddments of black felt for the eyelashes
Oddments of felt for the eyelids in a matching colour to the fur fabric

Whiskers Horsehair

Toy filling

Clothes
Male rabbit's pyjamas
A piece of striped material, flannelette would be suitable, 44.4cm (17½in) × 55.2cm (21¾in)
One small white tassel – a tassel from lampshade trimming would be about the right size

Female rabbit's nightdress
Small patterned cotton print material 35.5cm (14in) × 36.8cm (14½in)

Trimming: 83.8cm (33in) of 3.8cm (1½in) wide broderie anglaise for the sleeve and bodice
Neck trimming: 50.8cm (20in) of 2.5cm (1in) wide broderie anglaise

Mob cap
Broderie anglaise 40.6cm (16in) × 12.7cm (5in)
Ribbon for nightdress and mob cap trimming: 1m (39in) of 2.5cm (1in) wide terylene ribbon, to tone with the nightdress and the patterned bed material

Nightdress/pyjama case bed
One piece of patterned material to measure 91.5cm (36in) × 50.8cm (20in)
One piece of broderie anglaise material for lining the case, 99.1cm (39in) × 50.8cm (20in)
Patterned or plain material for the bed frill 177.4cm (70in) × 6.4cm (2½in)
Trimming for the top bedcover 101.6cm (40in) × 2.5cm (1in) wide

CONSTRUCTION
Cut out all the pattern pieces as listed.

Adult rabbits' heads Make the adult rabbits' heads as per the instructions for the head of the rabbit glove puppet (p. 60) with the exception of the eyes, which are made by stitching a felt eyelash piece to the bottom straight edge of each felt eyelid. The eyelids are then ladder stitched to each rabbit head (see colour plate to aid correct placing).

Body Identical for both rabbits.
With the right sides facing, place the two body pieces together. Pin then backstitch around the outside edge, leaving the top neck edge open. Turn to the right side and stuff. Gather the neck edge, adding more filling prior to closing to produce a firm base for the head. Ladder stitch the head to the body.

Arms See Diagram 20 for size. Cut four. With the right sides facing, place together in pairs; pin then backstitch around the outside edge, leaving the short straight edge open. Turn to the right side and stuff. Gather the open end, pull up and close. Make all the arms in the same way. Lay to one side.

Female rabbit's nightdress Cut a piece of small patterned material to measure 35.5cm (14in) × 14cm (5½in). Turn a narrow hem on both the long sides. With the right sides facing, fold in half, and stitch the 14cm (5½in) edges together. Turn to the

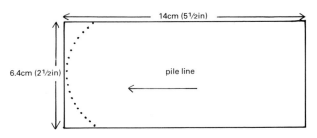

Diagram 20   Arm of rabbit nightdress case (curve one end for the hand)

right side and place on the body. Gather the top and bottom hems to fit the body, pull up and fasten off.

Sleeves
Cut two sleeve pieces 22.9cm (9in) × 12.7cm (5in). Turn a hem on one long side and add 3.8cm (1½in) wide broderie anglaise trimming to the other. With the right sides facing, fold in half and stitch the 12.7cm (5in) edges together. Turn to the right side. Gather the plain hemmed side, pull up tightly and fasten off.

Insert a prepared arm into the sleeve, leaving 5cm (2in) protruding beyond the sleeve end. Gather the end of the broderie anglaise trimmed sleeve and pull up tightly to fit the arm; put a few holding stitches and work round a second time, stitching the sleeve end to the arm. Make the other sleeve and attach the second arm in the same way.

On either side of the nightdress bodice cut a 3.8cm (1½in) slit. Fold in the raw edges. Insert the gathered end of a sleeve into each slit and stitch into place. This method of arm and sleeve insertion resembles stitched hinging; the arm hangs loosely in the attached sleeve and this produces flexibility so that the arms may be placed around the baby rabbit in the nightdress case bed.

Bodice trimming
Stitch two pieces of 14cm (5½in) × 2.5cm (1in) broderie anglaise trimming to the front of the

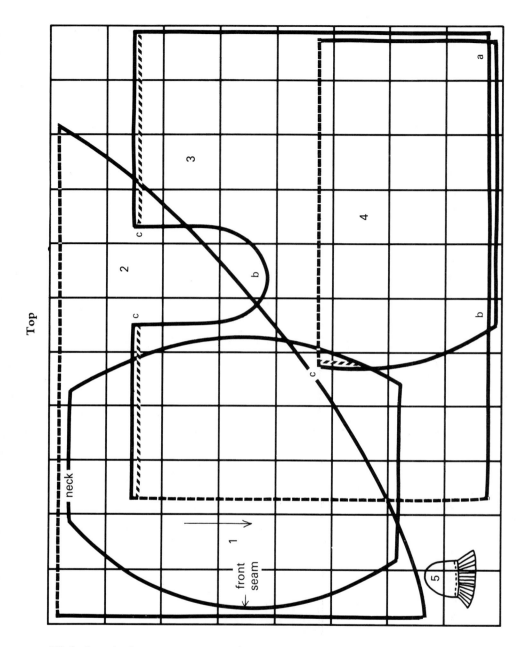

Nightdress/pyjama case pattern pieces

1 Body: cut two in fur fabric (one reversed) for each adult rabbit.

2 Nightcap: cut one in stripped material, for example flannelette.

3 Pyjama jacket: cut one in striped material.

4 Sleeves: cut two in striped material. Fold each sleeve back 2.5cm (1in) to form a cuff.

5 Eyelids and lashes: cut the top curved piece twice in felt to tone with the body fur fabric. Cut the lashes in black felt and cut as indicated. Reverse pattern for each eye.

The arms for each rabbit are four pieces of fur fabric, each measuring 6.4cm (2½in) wide × 14cm (5½in) long; curve one end of each piece for the paws (see Diagram 20).

bodice, starting at the centre front neck edge and opening out either side of the body front seam placing, to a finished width of 5cm (2in) at the bottom of the bodice. Finish by turning under the raw edges.

Neck trimming

Cut a piece of broderie anglaise trimming 50.8cm (20in) × 2.5cm (1in). Gather and pull up to fit around the neck. Fasten off at the back.

Mob cap

Cut a piece of broderie anglaise material 40.6cm (16in) × 12.7cm (5in). Hem both long sides. With the right sides facing, fold in half and stitch the 12.7cm (5in) edges together. Turn to the right side. Gather one long edge and pull up tightly. Fasten off. Run a gathering thread through the opposite edge, approximately 2.5cm (1in) from the hemmed edge. Pull up slightly and place the mob cap on the rabbit's head.

Cut a slit on either side for the ears, and turn in the raw edges. Pull up the gathering to fit the head just below the ear bases. Cut the ribbon in half and, with each piece, tie a small bow leaving long ribbon tail ends, and stitch one bow to the top of the mob cap at the centre back, and the second bow to the front of the dress under the neck frill.

Male rabbit's pyjamas

Jacket

Hem the bottom and front edges.

Sleeves

Hem the short straight edges. With the right sides facing, fold in half, and stitch the edges together from (a) to (b). Turn to the right side. Gather the shaped top of each sleeve slightly, where indicated. Insert and stitch the sleeves into the jacket armhole. Turn a hem on the top edge of the jacket and, using small running stitches, gather this top edge, also including the top of each sleeve; pull up slightly but do not fasten off.

Place the jacket on to the rabbit body and pull the gathering until it fits the rabbit neck with the front edges meeting; fasten off. Insert a prepared arm into each sleeve, as for the female rabbit, and stitch around the hemmed sleeve ends, attaching the sleeves to the arms.

Collar

Cut a piece of material 20.4cm (8in) × 3.8cm (1½in). Turn a 0.7cm (¼in) hem all round the outside edges. Place around the neck, stitch together at the top centre front and attach to the jacket to hold in place.

Nightcap

Turn a 1.3cm (½in) hem along the bottom straight edge. With the right sides facing, fold the nightcap in half and stitch the long edges together. Turn to the right side. Attach the tassel to the top point of the nightcap. Cut a 5cm (2in) slit for the ear in the right-hand side of the nightcap, approximately 2cm (¾in) up from the bottom edge. Turn in the raw edges. Place the nightcap on the rabbit's head with the right ear through the slit. Fold down the top point of the nightcap, behind the ear, to meet the bottom edge at the side of the head, and stitch to hold.

Nightdress case bed (see Diagram 21) With the patterned piece of material 91.5cm (36in) × 50.8cm (20in) wrong side uppermost, turn a 2.5cm (1in) hem all round the outside edge and tack (baste) to hold. With the right side of the 99.1cm (39in) × 50.8cm (20in) broderie anglaise material uppermost, lay this on to the wrong side of the patterned material and fold in a hem around one short and two long sides, leaving 1.3cm (½in) of the patterned 2.5cm (1in) hem showing; tack into place. The one short end is left open with 5cm (2in) of the broderie anglaise protruding – this will be the sheet turnback later.

Machine or hand stitch the broderie anglaise to the patterned material, leaving the sheet end open to enable stuffing to be inserted; remove the tacking. Hem around the protruding 5cm (2in) sheet fold-over, making sure that the hems will be underneath when the sheet is folded over the patterned bed.

Stuff the pillow end of the case to a pillow size of 25.4cm (10in) deep. Stitch across both the pillow and the bed together to hold the stuffing in place and to make a division between the pillow and the bed. Lightly stuff the bed part next – this should measure 28cm (11in) long; stitch across to hold the filling in place. Stitch across the bedcover to close, under the sheet turnback. Fold the remaining 35.5cm (14in) of patterned material back over the bed part and tack in place, leaving the right side open. Fold the sheet end over the cover.

Frill

Take a piece of the patterned material 177.4cm (70in) × 6.4cm (2½in) and stitch a narrow hem on one long and two short sides. Gather the remaining long edge to fit the patterned cover on two short and one long side. Tack then stitch around the cover edge, stitching through both the frill and the base of the case on one side and also the bottom edge, leaving the right side open to enable the insertion of the nightclothes and the top open for the rabbits.

Stitch a piece of broderie anglaise trimming, measuring approximately 101.6cm (40in) × 2.5cm (1in), around the bed, going over the frill gathering but omitting the top edge of the bed, which will be covered by the sheet turnback.

Add a piece of Velcro or a snap fastener to the left-hand side of the male rabbit and the right-hand side of the female rabbit, and place the other halves of the fastenings on either side of the base of the bed. To gauge the exact position, place the rabbits in the bed, with the male rabbit on the right-hand side facing inwards and the female rabbit on the left-hand side facing towards the male rabbit; mark where the fastening is required, remove the rabbits and stitch the fastenings into place. Tuck the baby rabbit between the arms of the mother.

Add snap fasteners or Velcro to the right-hand open side of the bed to enable closing when the child's nightclothes are inside.

Finally, stitch the remaining corner of the bedcover, on the open side, to the bed base. If the broderie anglaise material has a soft texture, and therefore the sheet does not stay in place, stitch across the sheet flap to the bedcover and then stitch the centre of the sheet at the top edge to the bed base.

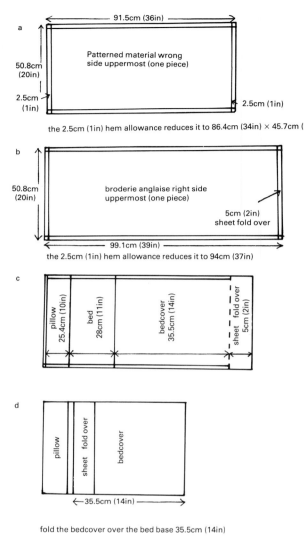

Diagram 21 Bed construction (not to scale)

11
RAG
BOOK

GRADING
Moderately difficult

TECHNIQUES
Machine appliqué

DESIGN BRIEF
A working rag book with zip, buttons, laces and a plait to teach the child co-ordination of hand movements

EVALUATION OF DESIGN BRIEF
Although this book was not intended for a very young child, it had to be strong enough to withstand constant wear, colourful enough to tempt the child to attempt the various tasks, and interesting – not just an abstract collection of pictures.

DEVELOPMENT OF DESIGN
It was decided to have a theme for this rag book. The subject of Indians is attractive to boys and girls and has a wide scope in content. Although only four page designs are given here for the rag book, the reader can add further pages as required. If inability to draw is a problem, this is easily overcome by looking through children's books and tracing suitable outline shapes. Children's painting books are an excellent source as they usually have very clear drawings. As with the matriochkas, the

actual stitching choice is left to the reader. Machine embroidery was used for the original rag book. Hand appliqué and embroidery, providing it is firm and strong, would also be suitable. Figures 12, 13, 14 and 15 will help readers in their choice of stitches. Decorate each page outline with a coloured thread to tone with the design colouring on that particular page.

MATERIALS REQUIRED
For each page a piece of unbleached calico 22.9cm (9in) × 60.9cm (24in)

Page 1: totem pole A piece of orange felt 7.6cm (3in) × 20.4cm (8in)
Fancy braid to tone 3.3cm (1¼in) × 20.4cm (8in)
Two orange coloured buttons 1.3cm (½in) diameter

Page 2: papoose Flesh coloured felt 7.6cm (3in) × 5cm (2in)
A piece of off-white short pile fur fabric 12.7cm (5in) × 17.8cm (7in)
A piece of tan coloured leather 12.7cm (5in) × 19.2cm (7½in)
Orange felt 7.6cm (3in) × 20.4cm (8in)

Page 3: Indian squaw Flesh coloured felt 12.7cm (5in) × 15.3cm (6in)
Light green felt 20.4cm (8in) × 7.6cm (3in)
Scraps of orange and yellow felt for the dress decoration
Cream coloured looped fringe 20.4cm (8in) × 2.5cm (1in)
Dark brown wool for the hair and plait
One elastic band to secure the plait
Braid for around the head 11.5cm (4½in) × 1.3cm (½in)

Page 4: wigwam Orange coloured felt 20.4cm (8in) × 20.4cm (8in)
Brown thin rolled braid for the wigwam supports 91.5cm (36in)
Brown zip 14cm (5½in)
Braid for trimming the wigwam 21.5cm (8½in) × 1.3cm (½in) wide

General Fabric paints or pens
Eyelet pliers with assorted coloured eyelets
One pair of long brown boot laces approximately 91.5cm (36in) each
Pinking shears
Copydex

CONSTRUCTION

Cut out all the pattern pieces as given. All the pages are made in the same way. Fold the 22.9cm (9in) × 60.9cm (24in) unbleached calico in half with the wrong sides facing to measure 22.9cm (9in) × 30.5cm (12in). Iron a crease on the top fold. The page is then opened out to its full size and the design is appliquéd to the front of the bottom half of the page.

After the design has been worked, the page is re-folded and the double pages joined together by decorative stitches worked 1.3cm (½in) in from the outside edges on two sides and the bottom only, omitting the top folded edge of the page. Cut round the three decorated sides with the pinking shears to produce a serrated edge.

Page 1: totem pole Open out the folded page and appliqué the totem pole in the centre of the lower page, 5.7cm (2½in) down from the top fold of the page. Using two different fancy stitches, work outline shapes around the totem pole – the first outline 2cm (¾in) away from the felt shape, and the second outline 1.3cm (½in) away from the first outline. Paint on the features.

Stitch the buttons in place on the totem pole where indicated on the pattern. Hem the ends of the 3.3cm (1¼in) × 20.4cm (8in) fancy braid to a finished length of 15.3cm (6in). Lay the braid over the buttons and mark where the button holes

should be. Remove the braid, cut and work the button holes. Place the buttons through the button holes and stitch the bottom edge of the braid to the centre of the totem pole base, approximately 0.7cm (¼in) up from the lower edge.

Re-fold the plain calico page behind the design with the wrong sides facing. Join the pages together as already instructed.

Page 2: papoose Stitch the baby's face behind the opening on the fur fabric and appliqué all together on to the calico page. Stitch over and around the fur fabric covered body part of the baby, to give the impression that the baby is wrapped in the fur. Paint on the features.

With the rougher side uppermost, lay the leather shape on top of the fur fabric, allowing an edging of the fur fabric to show around the baby's face. Punch three pairs of holes either side of the slit in the leather. Appliqué the orange felt strips either side of the leather shape and at the bottom, as shown on the pattern. Glue narrow bands of felt across the leather, where indicated, and stitch the ends to the side strips. Thread a boot-lace through the holes and tie at the top. Fold the page in half and join together as already instructed.

Page 3: Indian squaw Appliqué the shoulder piece in place first, with the bottom edge of the shoulder felt 9cm (3½in) up from the bottom edge of the

![Rag book page 1: totem pole] **Figure 12.** Rag book page 1: totem pole

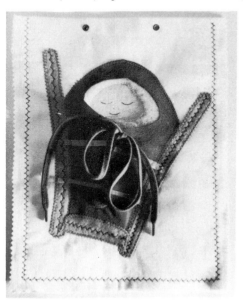

Figure 13. Rag book page 2: papoose

page. Stitch around the outside edge of the face piece and appliqué to the page, leaving two small openings on either side where indicated on the pattern. Paint on the features.

Appliqué the orange and yellow shapes on to the top of the dress, then appliqué the dress piece across the shoulders, 0.7cm (¼in) down from the chin. Stitch the braid fringe across the bottom of the dress, turning in the raw ends neatly.

Hair
Cut enough strands of knitting wool to cover the head front when laid together; the length, including the plait, should be 50.8cm (20in). Keeping the strands of wool flat, and working to the shape of the pattern, insert one group of the wool ends behind the face piece on the left-hand side where indicated (a). Stitch around the outside of the head shape to hold the hair in place until you reach the centre of the head. Stitch a centre parting. Continue to stitch the wool around the outside of the head shape to the opening at the opposite side of the head.

Cut several strands of wool measuring 3.8cm (1½in) and fold round the hair to hold together; insert the ends into the opening (b) and stitch to hold in place. Plait the remaining length of hair to the required finished length of 17.8cm (7in) and secure with an elastic band. Trim the ends. Stitch the hairband in place.

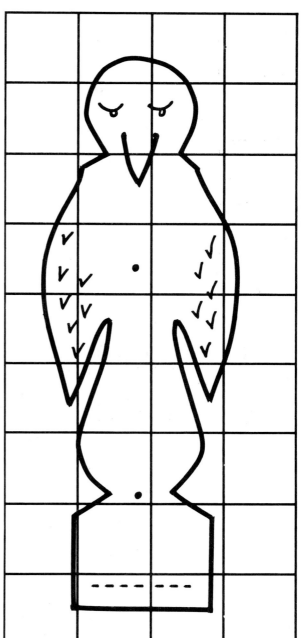

Figure 14. Rag book page 3: Indian squaw

Rag book pattern pieces

Page 1: totem pole: cut one totem pole piece in orange felt, and also a piece of toning fancy braid 2cm (¾in) wide × 20.4cm (8in) long.

53

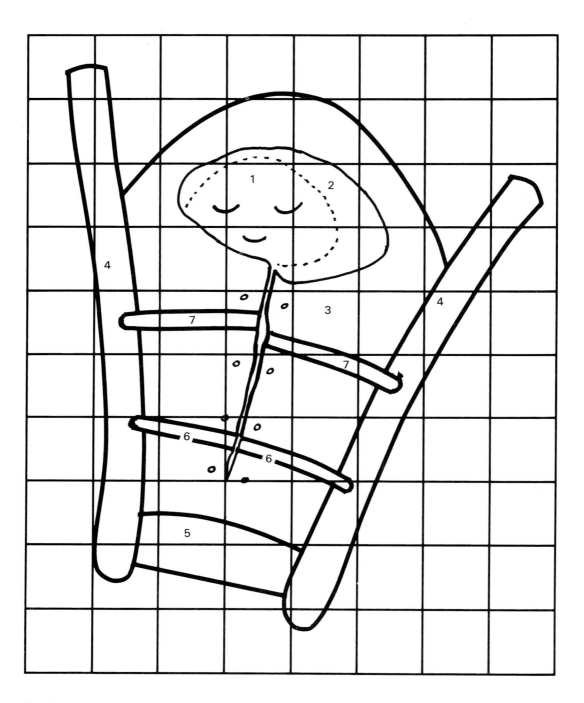

Page 2: papoose
1 Cut one face piece in flesh coloured felt.
2 Cut one piece of off-white fur fabric to the size of the inner dotted line, with the face oval cut out.
3 One piece of brown leather with the face window cut out and a slit down the centre.

4 Cut two strips of orange felt 20.4cm (8in) × 4cm (¾in).
5 Cut one strip of orange felt 7.6cm (3in) × 2.5cm (1in).
6 Cut one 10.3cm (4in) strip of orange felt and cut in half.
7 Cut one 11.5cm (4½in) strip of orange felt and cut in half.

Page 3: Indian squaw
Cut the face and shoulders in flesh coloured felt.
Cut the hairband in patterned braid.
Cut the dress in light green felt.
Cut the shapes on the dress in orange and yellow felt.
Lines on the edge of the dress indicate the fringe placing.

Figure 15. Rag book page 4: wigwam

bottom edge of the wigwam with 1.3cm (½in) wide braid. The wigwam can be left empty or, if preferred, the figure drawings given can be copied on to the calico prior to adding the wigwam. To enable the correct placing of the figures, lightly draw the wigwam shape onto the calico page in pencil. Fabric paints or pens are suitable for drawing the figures, or pencil can be used and the figure outlines embroidered. Appliqué the wigwam to the page. Fold the page in half and treat as the other pages.

Book page construction Using the pliers with the metal eyelets, make a hole on either side of the centre of each page 0.7cm (¼in) down from the top fold, the distance between the holes approximately 7cm (2¾in). Thread the ends of the remaining boot-lace through the eyelets on every page and tie in a bow at the front of the book.

Page 4: wigwam Cut four supports from the rolled braid each measuring 22.9cm (9in). Lay where indicated on the pattern (they will be underneath the wigwam) with an 11.5cm (4½in) space at the centre base and crossing over at the top where they protrude from the wigwam. Stitch the supports to the page. Stitch the zip in place to join the two sides of the wigwam front. Trim the

Embroidery pattern for inside wigwam (full size)

Page 4: wigwam
Cut one whole wigwam shape in orange coloured felt.
Cut two top wing shapes in the same coloured felt.

12
RABBIT GLOVE PUPPET, BABY AND PERAM-BULATOR

SIZE
Height 53.3cm (21in)

GRADING
Moderately difficult

TECHNIQUES
Adding legs to a glove puppet

DESIGN BRIEF
The use of the rabbit pattern extended to a soft toy with movement and maximum play value.

EVALUATION OF DESIGN BRIEF
Movement in a soft toy is manipulative rather than mechanical, hence the choice of a glove puppet with legs to simulate further movement. The maximum play value was achieved by the toy pram containing a baby rabbit.

Figure 16.   Rabbit glove puppet, baby and perambulator

MOTHER RABBIT

MATERIALS REQUIRED

For the glove puppet, white short pile fur fabric 55.9cm (22in) × 55.9cm (22in)

One pair of 14mm blue safety lock eyes

Pink felt for the ear linings 12.7cm (5in) × 11.5cm (4¼in)

White felt for half of the tail piece 7cm (2¾in) × 4.5cm (1¾in)

Horsehair for whiskers

Stranded embroidery silk for the nose and mouth markings

Toy filling

Clothes

Pantaloons
94cm (37in) of 20.4cm (8in) wide broderie anglaise trimming (this type of trimming has a pattern along one edge and a raw edge opposite)

Petticoat
Broderie anglaise 58.4cm (23in) × 12.7cm (5in)
Narrow broderie anglaise trimming 58.4cm (23in)

Dress and bonnet
Patterned or striped cotton material 91.5cm (36in) × 41.9cm (16½in)
Ricrac trimming for the dress bodice 25.4cm (10in)
1m (39in) of 2.5cm (1in) wide ribbon for the bonnet ties

Shoes
Felt to tone with the dress material 19.2cm (7½in) × 13.4cm (5¼in)
Two small buttons

CONSTRUCTION

Cut out the pattern pieces as listed.

The head Construct as for the jack-in-the-box rabbit, but placing the ears facing forward; whilst this is not anatomically correct, it adds to the appeal of this dressed puppet.

Puppet glove Construct as for the jack-in-the-box rabbit. The tail is made half in fur fabric and half in white felt.

The legs Cut two pieces of the fur fabric to measure 14cm (5½in) × 21cm (8¼in). Take one of the pieces and, with the right sides facing, fold in half lengthways. Backstitch the outside edges together leaving one short end open. Turn to the right side and stuff firmly. Ladder stitch the opening to close. Treat the other leg piece in the same way.

Pantaloons Cut two pieces of the broderie anglaise trimming to measure 17.8cm (7in) × 20.4cm (8in). With the right sides facing and the patterned edge placed at the bottom, cut up the centre of the material from the bottom edge for 14cm (5½in). Turn a hem at the top edge of each piece. Seam the side edges together and also the centre edges together. Turn to the right side.

Insert one of the prepared legs into a pantaloon leg leaving approximately 4.5cm (1¾in) of the leg protruding from the bottom of the pantaloon. Gather around the pantaloon leg 3.8cm (1½in) up from the bottom edge, and pull up the gathering to fit the leg; work a holding stitch, then stitch around a second time attaching the pantaloon leg to the fur fabric one. Fasten off. Treat the other leg in the same way.

Place the top front and back hems on the pantaloons together and overstitch across the front of the glove body 8.3cm (3¼in) from the bottom edge of the glove. The legs hang in the pantaloons and are therefore easy to manipulate.

Petticoat Cut a piece of broderie anglaise 58.4cm (23in) × 12.7cm (5in). Hem one long edge and add narrow broderie anglaise trimming. With the right sides facing, fold in half and stitch the 12.7cm (5in) edges together. Turn to the right side. Turn under a hem on the other long edge and gather to fit the glove body; work a holding stitch, then stitch around a second time attaching the top of the petticoat to the glove body at the waist.

Dress skirt Cut a piece of the patterned material to measure 91.5cm (36in) × 15.3cm (6in). Turn a hem on one long edge. With the right sides facing, fold in half and join the 15.3cm (6in) edges together. Turn to the right side. Turn in the top long edge and gather loosely to fit the puppet glove waist. Fasten off.

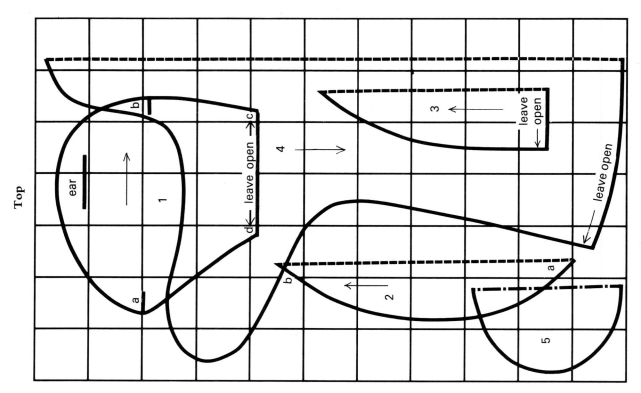

Rabbit glove puppet pattern pieces

1 Head: cut two in short pile fur fabric (one reversed).
2 Head gusset: cut one in short pile fur fabric.
3 Ears: cut two in short pile fur fabric. Cut two in felt for ear linings.

4 Rabbit glove: cut two in short pile fur fabric (one reversed).
5 Tail: cut one in fur fabric, and one in felt; join together to form a circle.

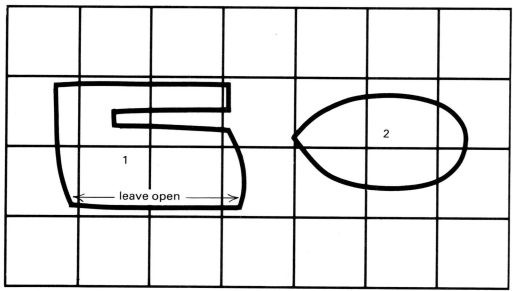

Shoe pattern piece

1 Cut four in felt.
2 Cut two in felt.

Bib Cut a piece of the patterned material 9.6cm (3¾in) × 15.3cm (6in). With the right sides facing fold in half to a size of 9.6cm (3¾in) × 7.6cm (3in). Stitch the side edges together leaving the bottom 9.6cm (3¾in) edge open. Turn to the right side. Fold in the open edges and stitch to the front of the dress skirt across the centre.

Arm and shoulder frill Cut a piece of the patterned material to measure 91.5cm (36in) × 9cm (3½in). Hem one long and two short edges. With the right sides of the material uppermost, fold in a hem on the opposite long edge and gather, pull up to measure 33cm (13in), and work a holding stitch.

Starting at one side of the bib at the waist, attach the frill to the bib side. Fasten off. Take the frill around the glove puppet shoulders to the opposite side of the bib and attach to the bib; fasten off at the waist. Take the centre of the bottom hem of the frill at the back of the glove and stitch to the top of the skirt for approximately 2.5cm (1in) across. Trim both sides and bottom of the bib front with ricrac trimming.

Bonnet Cut a 15.3cm (6in) diameter circle in the patterned material; turn in the outer edge and gather slightly. Stuff lightly and pull up the gathering stitches until the gathered edge of the circle measures 7.6cm (3in) in diameter. Fasten off.

Frill Cut a piece of the patterned material to measure 48.2cm (19in) × 17.8cm (7in). With the right sides of the material facing, fold in half lengthways. Stitch each pair of open side edges together leaving the long edge open. Turn to the right side, fold in the long edges and gather; pull up to 17.8cm (7in). Fasten off.

The brim is attached to half of the circle gathering line, 2.5cm (1in) on either side of the ears from one side of the head, across to the other, leaving two 5cm (2in) gaps at the top of the head where the ears are placed, so that the bonnet fits neatly over the ears.

Cut the ribbon in half. Make a 7.6cm (3in) loop in one end of a piece, and stitch to the outside of the bonnet frill at the side 1.3cm (½in) from the front edge. Hem the opposite raw end of the ribbon. Treat the second ribbon tie in the same way.

Shoes Cut out the pattern pieces as listed. Take two side pieces and stitch the back edges together and also the front edges. Insert a sole and backstitch in place. Turn to the right side, and stuff the toe of the shoe.

Place the shoe on to a leg and fold the straps around the front of the leg until obtaining a firm fit. Trim any excess strap. Place one strap end over the other and stitch together. Sew a button over the join. Stitch the top edge of the shoe to the leg to hold the shoe in place and to prevent the shoe falling off when the puppet is walking. Treat the other shoe in the same way.

BABY RABBIT

SIZE
Height 11.5cm (4½in)

MATERIALS REQUIRED
Fur fabric – short pile 28cm (11in) × 19.2cm (7½in)
One pair of 10mm safety lock eyes
Toy filling
Horsehair for whiskers
Stranded embroidery cotton

Figure 17. Baby rabbit

61

CONSTRUCTION

Cut out all the pattern pieces as listed.

BODY

With the right sides facing, pin the body pieces together inserting the stomach gusset between (c–d) and the head gusset between (a–b). Backstitch around the outside edge, leaving a stuffing opening where indicated on the pattern. Turn to the right side.

Insert the safety lock eyes using Figure 17 as a guide to placing them, making sure that the eyes are not too far back. Stuff the body firmly. Close the stuffing opening using ladder stitching.

EARS

Place one fur fabric and one felt pattern piece together with the fur fabric right side facing the felt. Pin then stitch around the outside edge, leaving the bottom straight edge open. Turn to the right side. Fold each outer corner of the bottom straight edge of the ear inwards to meet at the centre of the ear base. Stitch to hold.

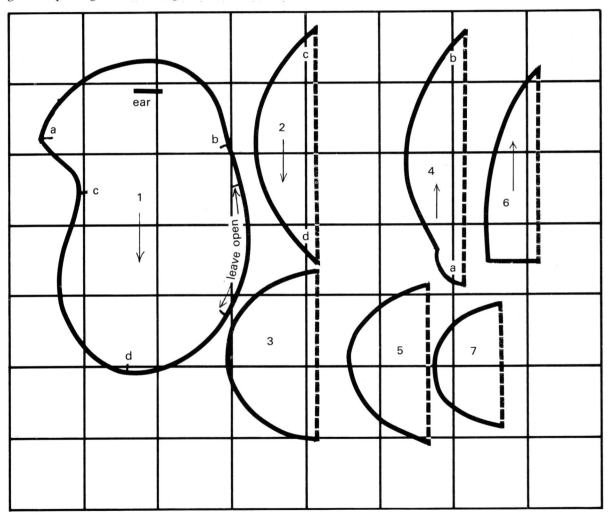

Baby rabbit pattern pieces

1 Body: cut two in fur fabric (one reversed).
2 Stomach gusset: cut one in fur fabric.
3 Tail: cut one in fur fabric.
4 Head gusset: cut one in fur fabric.
5 Feet: cut two in fur fabric.
6 Ears: cut two in fur fabric, two in felt.
7 Paws: cut two in fur fabric.

Prepare the other ear in the same way and then ladder stitch the ears in place on the head. A reference to the previous book may be useful for the ear construction and application.

PAWS AND FEET
Each comprises a fur circle gathered around the outside edge, with the gathering pulled up slightly. Each fur circle is stuffed and the gathering pulled up tightly to form a ball, then fastened off. The stuffed circles are then ladder stitched into place. Two paws and two feet are prepared and applied in this way. Refer to Figure 17 to aid the correct placing.

MOUTH AND WHISKERS
The mouth is embroidered in three strands of stranded embroidery cotton (see Diagram 29); and the whiskers are made from horsehair. Take a needle threaded with the horsehair into one side of the nose (see Figure 17 for position) and out of the other. Secure by working a few stitches, then take back out at the first point. Work another whisker in the same way, only slightly higher on the nose. Repeat, in reverse, for the whiskers on the other side of the nose.

PERAMBULATOR

SIZE
Length 25.4cm (10in)

TECHNIQUES
Adapting a bought basket into a toy perambulator

MATERIALS REQUIRED
A purchased woven basket. The original perambulator was made using a basket with a 15.3cm (6in) × 10.3cm (4in) base, and curving out at each end to a finished length of 25.4cm (10in) × 20.4cm (8in) across the centre of the basket. The material quantities are given for a basket of this size, but can easily be adapted to the size of the basket available.
A piece of handle cane 33cm (13in) long
Strong wire or staking cane 48.2cm (19in)
Strong tape to bind wire or cane
A piece of plywood cut to fit the oval base of the basket
Four screws to attach the plywood base to the wooden wheel axles
A piece of 2cm (¾in) × 2cm (¾in) wood

measuring 24.1cm (9½in), cut in half for the wheel axles
Four wooden wheels 5cm (2in) diameter
Four 2.5cm (1in) × 10s R/H (round headed) black japanned screws, and four washers; ordinary screws can be used (as in Figure 18) but tend to have rather sharp edges which have to be smoothed down

Mattress, pillow and sheet Broderie anglaise 44.5cm (17½in) × 41.9cm (16½in)

Pram hood and cover Small patterned cotton material 91.5cm (36in) × 52cm (20½in)
Toy filling

CONSTRUCTION
Screw the oval inner plywood base to the axles, by placing the base inside the basket and screwing through the wooden base, then the basket base, and into the wooden axles placed under either end of the oval basket base (see Figure 19). Fix a wheel on to the end of each axle with a washer between each wheel and axle.

Handle Taper each end of a piece of handle cane measuring 33cm (13in). Insert each end into the weaving at one end of the basket, leaving a 10.3cm (4in) space in between. Press the tapered ends well down into the weaving beside an upright cane.

Mattress Cut two pieces of broderie anglaise 15.3cm (6in) × 20.4cm (8in), curve each corner to form an oval. With the right sides facing, stitch the outside edges together leaving an opening to facilitate turning. Turn to the right side. Lightly, but evenly, stuff and close the opening. Place inside the pram.

Pillow Cut a piece of broderie anglaise to measure 12.7cm (5in) × 22.9cm (9in). With the right sides facing, fold in half to reduce in size to 12.7cm (5in) × 11.5cm (4½in). Stitch the outside edges together on one long and one short side. Turn to the right side. Lightly, but evenly, stuff then close the opening. Place in the pram.

Sheet Cut a piece of broderie anglaise to measure 29.2cm (11½in) × 21.5cm (8½in) and hem around the outside edges. Place in the pram with the longer measurement across the pram to give enough length to tuck under the mattress.

Figure 18. Perambulator: view inside

Figure 19. Perambulator: view underneath

Cover In the patterned cotton material cut a piece 25.4cm (10in) × 17.8cm (7in). Leaving one long edge straight, curve around the other edges to the shape of the basket. Turn a small hem around the outside edge.

Frill Cut a piece of the patterned material to measure 73.7cm (29in) × 7.6cm (3in). With the wrong sides facing, fold in half lengthways. Turn in the raw edges and gather to fit the curved edges on the cover; stitch in place. The top straight edge of the cover remains untrimmed and the sheet is folded over the top.

Hood Cover either a 48.2cm (19in) length of strong wire or weaving cane, first with adhesive tape, then bind with ordinary tape, stitching to hold securely in place. Cut a piece of the patterned material to measure 91.5cm (36in) × 19.2cm (7½in). Turn a narrow hem on both short and one long side. Gather the long hemmed edge and pull up; stitch the two ends of the gathering together.

Due to the bulk of the cotton material, the gathering will not pull up to close but there will be a remaining circle of gathering approximately 3.8cm (1½in) in diameter. This is the back of the hood. Stitch the join in the gathering to the top woven edge at the centre back of the basket.

Turn a 2.5cm (1in) hem on the long raw edge of the material, leaving a channelway to enable the prepared cane or wire to be inserted. Without pulling too hard on the material with the inserted wire, press the covered wire ends into either side of the basket, placing them well down into the weaving, if possible beside an upright stake. Stitch to hold.

The gathered hood is held firmly across the front of the pram by the covered wire. As a gauge to the correct placing of the wire ends, the hood material edges should follow round the top edge of the basket. If pulled too tightly, there will be gaps at each side of the pram between the material and the top edge of the basket. Cotton will hold its shape, but if a lighter weight material is used, it may be necessary to secure the hood edges to the basket with stitching.

13
DOLL'S HOUSE DUCK FAMILY

GRADING
Easy

TECHNIQUES
The handling of small toys and adapting toy techniques to a miniature form

DESIGN BRIEF
A family to a small scale using felt as the main fabric medium

EVALUATION OF DESIGN BRIEF
The patterns are given in full size. When making these toys, the toymaker will experience the vast difference between a small and large toy. It is necessary to think in miniature. All stitching must be small. Toy filling must be used in very small quantities at a time.

CHOICE OF MATERIALS
Felt was chosen as this is an easy fabric to work with and greatly assists the handling of a small article. These toys could make the basis for a group project.

MATERIALS REQUIRED
These toys can be made from oddments of felt with the addition of trimmings.
Coloured felts used to make the original toys: green, yellow, dark green, orange, peach, black, fawn, brown and white

Felt trimming
Broderie anglaise
Dainty flowered nylon
Brown Turabast or raffia
Toy filling
Bottle top
Oval or square piece of hardboard or 0.7cm (1/4in) ply, size approximately 30.5cm (12in) × 22.9cm (9in)

CONSTRUCTION
Cut out the pattern pieces as listed.

Adult duck's body Both bodies are identical. Place the two body pieces together; overstitch round the outside edge using matching thread, leave the base open and stuff well, then overstitch the opening to close.

Adult duck's feet For each foot, place the pieces together in pairs, stitch around the outside edge leaving a part of one side open to stuff, then overstitch all round to close. Ladder stitch to base of body (see Diagram 22).

Adult duck's wings For each duck cut out two wings. If the felt being used is rather lightweight, strength can be added by using iron-on Vylene on the back of each wing. Attach the wing where indicated on Diagram 23.

Adult eyes Cut two small circles of black felt and sew into position (see colour plate).

Adult beak Cut two pieces of orange coloured felt for each bird to the size of the beak shape on the pattern outline. Overstitch around the outside edge, leaving the straight edge open to enable the beak to be slipped on to the beak shape of the body. Stitch to hold.

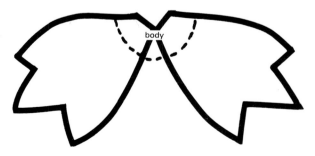

Diagram 22   Position of feet under the duck body

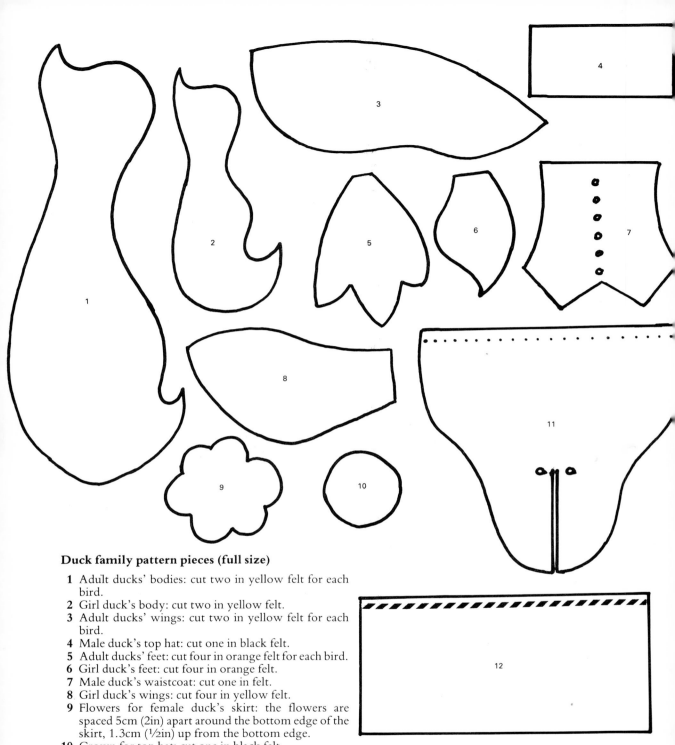

Duck family pattern pieces (full size)

1 Adult ducks' bodies: cut two in yellow felt for each bird.
2 Girl duck's body: cut two in yellow felt.
3 Adult ducks' wings: cut two in yellow felt for each bird.
4 Male duck's top hat: cut one in black felt.
5 Adult ducks' feet: cut four in orange felt for each bird.
6 Girl duck's feet: cut four in orange felt.
7 Male duck's waistcoat: cut one in felt.
8 Girl duck's wings: cut four in yellow felt.
9 Flowers for female duck's skirt: the flowers are spaced 5cm (2in) apart around the bottom edge of the skirt, 1.3cm (½in) up from the bottom edge.
10 Crown for top hat: cut one in black felt.
11 Male duck's coat: cut one in black felt.
12 Female duck's bonnet: cut one in felt. Cut two bonnet ties in felt 12.7cm (5in) long × 0.7cm (¼in) wide.
13 Girl duck's bonnet: cut one in felt.

Female duck's apron: cut a piece of felt to measure 20.4cm (8in) × 5.7cm (2¼in).

Apron ties: cut two pieces of felt 12.7cm (5in) × 0.7cm (¼in).

DRESSING THE MALE DUCK

Waistcoat Sew the waistcoat to the front of the body where indicated on Diagram 23.

Bow tie Using a strip of 0.7cm (¼in) wide white felt, make a tiny bow tie. Trim the length to fit as shown on the diagram, and stitch in place.

Coat Fold over the collar as indicated by the dotted line on the pattern; stitch on either side of duck to cover the end stitching just below the bow tie. Cut a 0.7cm (¼in) × 0.7cm (¼in) square of white felt. Snip along one edge to make a fringe. Roll it up, stitch to hold and trim to make a tiny flower. Sew to the lapel of the coat.

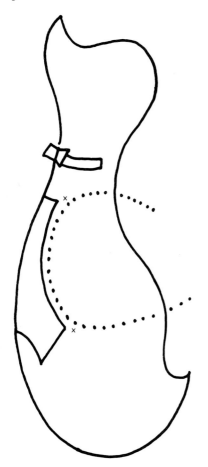

Diagram 23 Placing of waistcoat on body. Stitch to body top at (x) across front of chest to opposite side. Stitch to secure to body at lower (x) just under wing on each side of body (dotted line indicates wing placing).

Top hat Fold hat piece no. 4 into a tube and overstitch the seam. Place this on to the centre of the hat piece no. 10 and stitch into place. Stuff the tube. Cut a circle of felt to fit the top of the tube and overstitch around the outside edge. Stab stitch the hat to the duck's head. Add a hatband composed of a strip of white felt 0.7cm (¼in) wide round the hat. Stitch to hold.

DRESSING THE FEMALE DUCK

Apron Gather the apron until it measures 10.3cm (4in); fasten off. Sew ties to each side. Cut four daisies and four centres, and stitch to skirt as shown in the colour plate.

Bonnet Gather where indicated on pattern to 5cm (2in); fasten off. Sew on the ties.

GIRL DUCK
Make the body in the same way as for adult ducks. The bonnet is made as for the adult duck, the size 5cm (2in) × 2cm (¾in). Gather to fit girl duck's neck. Make a tiny bow in felt and sew to the front under her chin.

Skirt Cut a piece of felt 15.3cm (6in) × 3.8cm (1½in). Gather to fit round the duck's waist, under the wings, and secure at the back. Make a tiny bow for the centre back at waist. Stitch into place.

Apron Cut in broderie anglaise trimming a strip 2.5cm (1in) wide × 5cm (2in) long. Sew to the front of the skirt, securing at the waist.

TREE
Cut a 15.3cm (6in) piece of wire, about the gauge of a size 13 knitting needle. Cut four more pieces for the branches measuring 5cm (2in), 7.6cm (3in), 8.3cm (3¼in), 9cm (3½in). Using narrow adhesive tape secure the four branches to one end of the 15.3cm (6in) wire. Starting at the base of the tree, secure one end of the dark brown Turabast or raffia, and bind by twisting the wire in the left hand, and holding the Turabast in the right hand. Take special care to bind very tightly where the branches join the main stem; continue to the end of one branch. Glue to hold and finish off the Turabast at the end of the branch. Taking each branch in turn, cover with the Turabast, glue and secure.

As a base to hold the tree upright, use a small bottle-top filled with self-hardening clay. The leaves on the original tree were cut from felt trimming; if not available, cut leaf shapes in various toned green felt oddments. The blossom on the tree was made out of scraps of dainty flowered pink nylon, gathered on one edge and pulled up to form rosettes. Broderie anglaise flower trimming is also suitable, each flower cut individually then glued on to the branches of the tree.

SWING
Cut a 20.4cm (8in) strip of pretty flowered trimming, attach at each end to one of the branches. Attach the duck to the swing by her wings.

GARDEN BASE
Whilst the base illustrated measured 30.5cm (12in) × 22.9cm (9in) × 0.7cm (¼in), any oddment of similar size would do. Cover the top with green felt, and glue a brown felt path in place using Copydex. Flowers are added cut from felt trimming or from oddments of felt. The edge all around the board can be trimmed with any pretty braid.

To keep the cost to a minimum when decorating the base, go through your needlework box to find suitable pieces to cut up for the flowers. Artificial or dried flowers can look most attractive, although not very durable when the doll's house garden is played with. Tiny plastic flowers last longer. The rosebush in the colour plate was a gift decoration.

It can add great play value if a large base is covered in green felt for the doll's house to stand on, then individual scenes of differing sizes and shapes can be made up so that the garden layout can be altered as required.

14
DOLL'S HOUSE MOUSE AND CRADLE

CRADLE SIZE
10.3cm (4in) long × height to top of canopy 7.6cm (3in)

MOUSE SIZE
Height 5cm (2in)

DESIGN BRIEF
A doll's house size bed with a small toy inside

MATERIALS REQUIRED
Mouse Felt 3.3cm (1¼in) × 4.5cm (1¾in)

Cradle

Pillow and cover
Felt 25.4cm (10in) × 17.8cm (7in)

Blanket
Felt 5.7cm (2¼in) × 3.3cm (1¼in)

Cradle trim
Lace 43.7cm (17in) long × 3.3cm (1¼in) wide

Canopy trim
Lace 20.4cm (8in) long × 7.6cm (3in) wide

Cradle cover
Lace 15.3cm (6in) long × 1.3cm (½in) wide

Mouse nightgown
Lace 12.7cm (5in) long × 2.5cm (1in) wide

Oddments of lace required to trim blanket and for the pillow rosette
Ribbon for bows on cradle: 0.95m (1yd) approximately 0.7cm (¼in) wide
Two pipe-cleaners
Small amount of toy filling
Black cotton for whiskers and eye embroidery
Copydex or similar latex-based adhesive

CONSTRUCTION
Cut out all the pattern pieces as listed.

Cradle base Using Copydex, glue the card base between the two felt base pieces. Do not take the adhesive right to the outside edge, as this must be free to enable it to be sewn to the cradle sides.

Cradle side Cut a piece of felt in the main colour approximately 22.9cm (9in) × 6.4cm (2½in). Fold this in half lengthways and place a pipe-cleaner cut to 22.9cm (9in) long in the fold, then stab stitch to hold the pipe-cleaner in place. Bend the enclosed pipe-cleaner to an oval to fit the oval base (a–b). Stitch together where (ab) seams meet. If it is not a neat fit to the oval base, which can happen if the felt stretches, then trim a little off the end prior to stitching the seams (ab) together.

Pin then overstitch the inside bottom edge of the cradle side to the base. When the overstitching is complete, cut small slits in the top loose side of the cradle at approximately 2.5cm (1in) intervals.

Cradle canopy Cut a piece of felt 15.3cm (6in) × 5cm (2in). Cut a pipe-cleaner to measure 15.3cm (6in) long. Lay the pipe-cleaner on one long side of

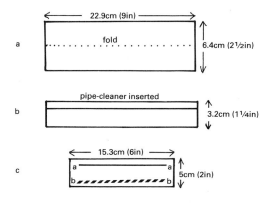

Diagram 24 Construction of cradle (not to scale). a) Cradle side. b) Cradle side folded. c) Cradle canopy

the felt and fold over the felt edge so that the pipe-cleaner is completely encased; stab stitch to hold the pipe-cleaner in place. Gather the opposite long edge using a small running stitch; pull up tightly and fasten both ends together.

Pin this canopy with the pipe-cleaner bent into an oval, with gathers at point (ab) on base and sides of the canopy at either side. Stitch this canopy to the cradle sides 1.3cm (½in) down from the top edge.

Gather a length of lace measuring 43.7cm (17in) long × 3.3cm (1¼in) wide to fit and cover the cradle sides. Stitch to the top edge of the cradle sides, just under the top edge. Take a piece of lace 20.4cm (8in) long × 7.6cm (3in) wide. Gather a 0.7cm (¼in) in from one long edge to fit the canopy front. Stitch to the front edge of the canopy just behind the covered pipe-cleaner, from one side to the other. Gather the opposite long edge 1.3cm (½in) in from the outside and pull in tightly to fit the gathered felt back of the canopy. This forms a rosette.

Make two small bows and sew to either side of the canopy; make one slightly larger one and sew this to the canopy in the centre of the gathered rosette.

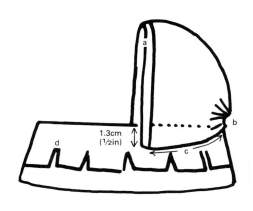

Diagram 25 a) Pipe-cleaner inserted around front edge. b) Back of hood gathers. c) Bottom edge of the canopy stitched to the side of the cradle 1.3cm (½in) down from the top edge. d) Felt edge cut to shape

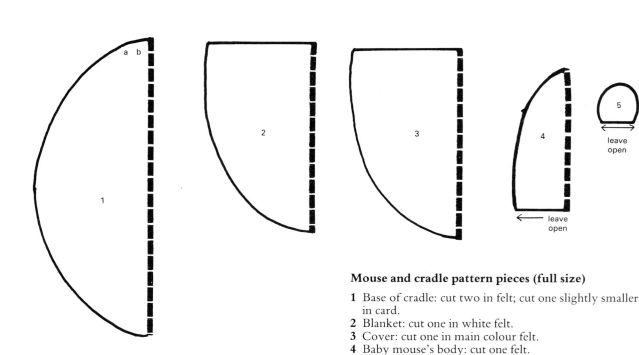

Mouse and cradle pattern pieces (full size)

1 Base of cradle: cut two in felt; cut one slightly smaller in card.
2 Blanket: cut one in white felt.
3 Cover: cut one in main colour felt.
4 Baby mouse's body: cut one felt.
5 Mouse ear: cut two in main body colour felt; cut two in pale pink for ear linings.

70

Diagram 26 a) Showing tail, ear and eye placing. b) Showing ear and whisker placing (dotted line indicates placing of a gathered strip of lace edging for the nightdress)

Bedclothes

Pillow

Fold a 5cm (2in) wide × 10.3cm (4in) deep piece of felt in half. Stitch together one short and one long side. Stuff firmly then close the remaining side. Gather a small piece of lace along one edge to make a rosette as decoration; pull up and stitch to the top left-hand corner of the pillow.

Blanket

Cut one pattern piece in white felt and trim along the top straight edge with narrow lace.

Cradle cover Cut one pattern piece in the main colour felt. Gather a 15.3cm (6in) × 1.3cm (½in) strip of lace and stitch to the curved edge of the cover a 0.7cm (¼in) in from the outside edge. Leave top straight edge untrimmed.

Mouse Cut one body piece in grey felt; fold in half on the long straight edge and overstitch around the outside curved edges together, leaving the base open to stuff. Stuff firmly. Cut a circle of grey felt to fit the base of the mouse body and overstitch into place.

Place one ear piece in body colour and one pale pink felt lining together and overstitch around the outside edge. Fold in half lengthways to form a folded ear. Make the other ear in the same way and secure to either side of the head at X. A French knot on either side of the nose point, where indicated on the body, is sufficient for the eyes. The whiskers are applied using cotton strands. The tail is a narrow strip of felt, or, if preferred, thin cord can be used.

Nightgown Gather a strip of lace 2.5cm (1in) wide × 12.7cm (5in) long to fit around the mouse body and stitch to hold at the centre of the back.

15
AWAKE/ASLEEP DOUBLE-ENDED RABBIT

GRADING
Moderately difficult

TECHNIQUES
Use and adaptation of a toy with a historical background (refer to Projects 12 and 16)

DESIGN BRIEF
Using the theme of the rabbit pattern to design a double-ended toy

EVALUATION OF DESIGN
The choice of a rabbit subject produced a slight problem due to the length of the ears which meant it thus required a longer skirt than would normally have been required.

MATERIALS REQUIRED
Rabbit heads and hands White short pile fur fabric 30.5cm (12in) × 36.8cm (14½in)

Ear linings Pink felt 10.3cm (4in) × 17.8cm (7in)

One pair of blue 14mm safety lock eyes
Oddments of white and black felt for the sleeping eyes

Whiskers Black horsehair

Black stranded embroidery silk for the feature marking

Bodies and arms Strong cotton material 40.6cm (16in) × 25.4cm (10in)
Material to dress one rabbit end 81.3cm (32in) × 55.9cm (22in)
Choose two patterns in colours which complement each other, one for each end of the toy. The rabbit pattern has the awake rabbit dressed in a day dress with a mob cap and apron, and the opposite end asleep rabbit wears a nightdress.

Apron and mob cap Taffeta, nylon, cotton or any suitable material 60.9cm (24in) × 25.4cm (10in)
Narrow ribbon for the apron ties 45.7cm (18in)

Trimmings Narrow lace trimming for the apron 94cm (37in)
Dress trimming for the awake rabbit 35.5cm (14in) of 2.5cm (1in) wide broderie anglaise
Narrow ribbon to tone with the dress 2m (78in)
Nightdress trimming for the asleep rabbit 30.5cm (12in) of 1.3cm (½in) wide frilled nylon or lace trimming

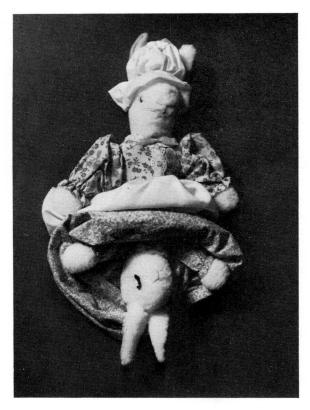

Figure 20. Awake/asleep double-ended rabbit

Hanging toys on pram cover

Rabbit nightdress case

Duck family

Rag book

Rabbit jack-in-the-box

Oddment of narrow ribbon for a small neck bow on the nightdress

Trimming for the bottom edge of the combined skirts

Gathered broderie anglaise trimming 78.7cm (31in) of 1.3cm (½in) wide; this type of trimming can be purchased already gathered on to a band

Toy filling

CONSTRUCTION

Cut out the pattern pieces as listed.

Make two complete rabbit heads using the rabbit glove puppet pattern and construct following the instructions for the jack-in-the-box rabbit. The one head has blue 14mm safety lock eyes inserted, the other head has felt sleeping eyes applied as the nightdress case rabbits. Stuff the heads firmly and gather the neck edges and close. The ear linings on both the rabbit heads is pale pink felt.

Rabbit body Cut two pieces of strong cotton material to measure 10.3cm (4in) × 12.7 (5in). Place together with the right sides facing. Remove two corners on the 10.3cm (4in) measurement, curving slightly for the shoulders. Stitch the outside edges together leaving the bottom straight edge open and a small opening for the stuffing on one side edge. Make a duplicate body piece. Join the two body pieces together round the waist leaving the opening at one side where indicated on the diagram. Turn to the right side. Stuff firmly and close the opening.

Dress/nightdress bodice Both bodices are made in the same way. Cut two pieces of the patterned material to measure 12.7cm (5in) × 15.3cm (6in). With the right sides facing, place together. Remove the corners on either side of the 12.7cm (5in) measurement and curve to fit the shoulder curves on the body.

Stitch the outside edges together leaving the bottom straight edge open. Turn to the right side and place on to one end of the stuffed body. Place the second bodice over the other end of the body piece. Turn in the material at the open ends of the bodices and stitch to the waist with the bottom hems meeting so that no gap appears through which the body would show.

Dress/nightdress skirt Cut a piece of patterned material 76.2cm (30in) × 43.7cm (17in). With the right sides facing, join the 43.7cm (17in) seams. Turn to the right side. Turn in the top edge of the skirt, and gather to fit the waist of the matching bodice and stitch to the body.

Make the other skirt in the same way. The raw edges on the skirts are left open at this stage.

Rabbit heads Ladder stitch to either end of the body, making sure that the sleeping head is on the material chosen for the nightdress and vice versa.

Arms The arms must swing up and down easily whichever end of the toy is being used, so stitch or lap hinging is used when applying the arms.

In strong cotton material cut four pieces measuring 10.3cm (4in) × 12.7cm (5in). Take one piece and, with the right sides facing, fold in half lengthways to measure 5cm (2in) × 12.7cm (5in). Stitch the outside edges together leaving one 5cm (2in) end open. Turn to the right sides.

If applying the arms by lap hinging, top stitch across the arm approximately 2.5cm (1in) from the top so that it remains free from toy filling when the arm is stuffed. Stuff the arm firmly and close. Make three more arms in the same way.

Hands In the white fur fabric cut four 9cm (3½in) diameter circles. For each hand gather around the outside edge of one circle; pull up slightly and insert a small quantity of toy filling. Insert one end of an arm into the circle and pull up the gathering to fit the arm; just prior to closing, add more toy filling if required. Work a holding stitch then stitch the hand to the arm. Make and apply all the hands in the same way. Lap hinge an arm to either side of the body piece at each end as indicated on the diagram.

Trim down the front of the bodice and round the neck of the awake rabbit with the broderie anglaise trimming. Tie a bow at the neck, centre front, and another bow, with long tails, at the waist of the skirt at the centre front. Trim the nightdress down the bodice front and around the neck with nylon or lace frilled trimming. Tie a small bow at the neck, centre front, below the frilled trimming.

Sleeves Cut two sleeves measuring 25.4cm (10in) × 12.7cm (5in) for each rabbit. Curve one end of each sleeve slightly. With the right sides of the material facing, fold in half lengthways and join the long edges together. Turn to the right side.

Turn in the top curved edge and gather to fit above the lap hinging on the arm, then, with the seam under the arm, stitch the sleeve to the body. Turn in the sleeve end and gather approximately 1.3cm (½in) from the sleeve edge; pull up to fit the arm just above the fur fabric hand. Treat all the sleeves in the same way.

Check that both skirt lengths are identical and that they cover the heads, including the long ears. Turn up a hem on each skirt and tack (baste) separately. Insert the gathered broderie anglaise trimming between the two skirt hems and stitch all together. The hem of the day dress on the awake rabbit is trimmed above the inserted broderie anglaise with narrow ribbon all around the skirt, with a small bow stitched to the centre of the hem at the front of the dress.

Mob cap Cut a piece of white material 60.9cm (24in × 17.8cm (7in). Hem one long edge. With the right sides facing, fold in half and stitch the side edges together. Turn to the right side. Fold in one long edge and gather tightly; fasten off. Fold under 5cm (2in) at the bottom raw edge and stitch to hold. Gather but do not pull up.

Place the cap on to the awake rabbit head and cut a slit on either side for the ears. Remove the cap and turn in the raw edges on the ear slits. Replace the cap on the rabbit head and pull up the gathering to fit the head just below the base of each ear. Fasten off. Tie a small bow leaving long ribbon tails and stitch to the top of the mob cap at the back.

Apron Cut a piece of white material to match the mop cap to measure 40.6cm (16in) × 25.4cm (10in). Turn a hem on one long and two short edges. Trim with narrow lace. Turn a hem on the remaining long edge and gather to 15.3cm (6in). Fasten off. Cut two pieces of narrow ribbon for the apron ties each measuring 22.9cm (9in). Turn in one end of each piece neatly. Make a 1.3cm (½in) loop on the other end of each piece and stitch to the apron on either side of the top gathering. Place around the waist of the awake rabbit.

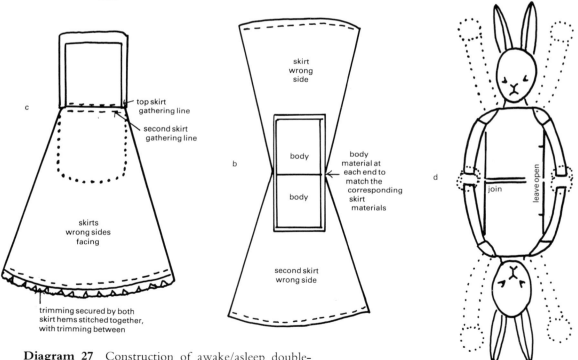

Diagram 27 Construction of awake/asleep double-ended rabbit

74

16
RABBIT JACK-IN-THE-BOX

SIZE
Extended height of rabbit 25.4cm (10in)

GRADING
Difficult

TECHNIQUES
Making a box and applying a spring

DESIGN BRIEF
A jack-in-the-box design with the concept of a soft toy

EVALUATION OF DESIGN BRIEF
It was obvious from the word 'soft' that, other than the metal spring, all the parts of this toy must be made using soft toy materials. When developing a design from a given brief, it is essential to note, and list, the main elements required, because otherwise it is easy to be misled and finish up with a design which does not comply with the original requirements.

If a ready-made box to the size required is available, this can be covered in felt. It is usually the case, however, that a toymaker decides to make a particular subject and is then thwarted by not having the required materials to hand, and thus a box must be made. For further details, refer to the sections on box construction and the jack-in-the-box in *The Techniques of Soft Toymaking*.

MATERIALS REQUIRED

Rabbit and baby A piece of short pile fur fabric 50.8cm (20in) × 46.3cm (18¼in)
A piece of white fur fabric for the tail 4.5cm (1¾in) × 7cm (2¾in)
Felt for the ear linings 17.8cm (7in) × 9cm (3½in)
One pair of 14mm safety lock eyes
One pair of 10mm safety lock eyes
Horsehair for the whiskers
Stranded embroidery silk for the mouth and nose markings
Lightweight toy filling
Terylene ribbon measuring 76.2cm (30in) × 2.5cm (1in) wide
Scraps of orange and green felt for the carrot

The box The finished size of the box illustrated is 12.7cm (5in) × 15.3cm (6in) × 12.7cm (5in). It is made of card panels covered in felt.
Light green felt for the outside of the box 63.5cm (25in) × 38.1cm (15in)
Dark brown felt for the inside of the box 63.5cm (25in) × 38.1cm (15in)
Strong card for the box panels: six pieces for the sides and two bases 15.3cm (6in) × 12.7 (5in) and one piece 16cm (6¼in) × 13.3cm (5¼in) for the lid
White lampshade braid 53.3cm (21in)

Box trimming
Oddments of various coloured felts
Broderie anglaise flower trimming
Lace flower trimming

Box fastening
Either a button and a loop of thin cord to hold the lid down, or a piece of Velcro (touch fastener) (as the scene around the box was grass and flowers from which the rabbit could pop out, the fastener was a covered wire bee, and the loop on the lid fastened around it to hold the lid shut)

The inner roll of a disposable kitchen towel
A spring sufficiently flexible to be easily pushed into the box but strong enough to press upwards and support the weight of the body construction

CONSTRUCTION
Cut out all the pattern pieces as listed.

Glove With the right sides of the material facing, pin then backstitch the outside edges together leaving the bottom straight edge open. Turn up a

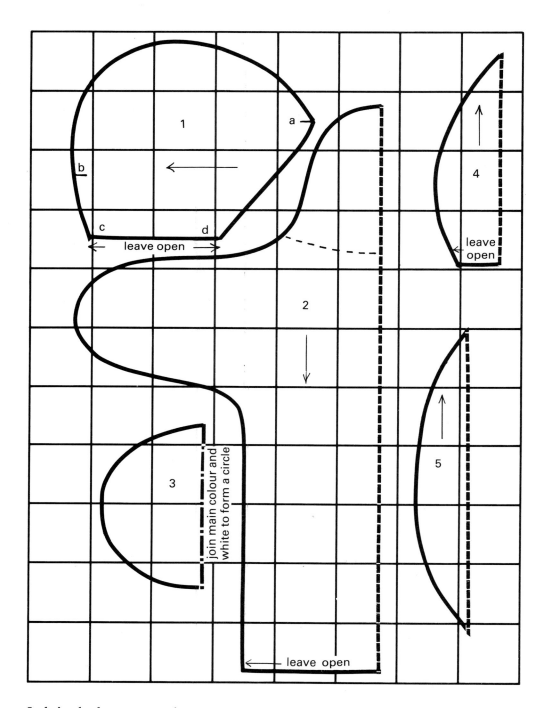

Jack-in-the-box pattern pieces

1 Head: cut two in fur fabric (one reversed).
2 Glove body: cut two in fur fabric (one reversed).
3 Tail: cut one in main colour fur fabric; cut one in white felt.

4 Ears:cut two in main colour fur fabric; cut two in felt for ear linings.
5 Head gusset: cut one in main colour fur fabric.

narrow hem on this bottom straight edge. Turn to the right side.

Lightly stuff the arms to add shaping. Place a few stitches through the arms from the front to the back of the glove to hold the filling in place, leaving the body of the glove completely empty.

Head With the right sides of the two side head pieces together, pin then backstitch from (d) on the neck edge to (a) at the nose. Insert the head gusset matching (a–b) on the gusset to (a–b) on both sides of the head. Pin then backstitch the gusset in place; on the second side continue stitching down to (c) at the neck edge, joining the back of head edges (b–c) together. Turn to right side. Insert the safety lock eyes.

Stuff the head and slightly gather the neck edge. Place the head on to the glove with the neck edge

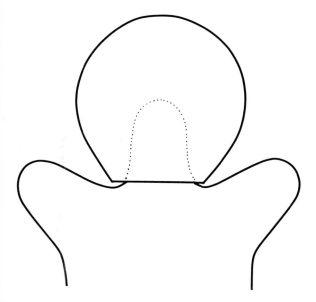

Diagram 28 Placing of head on to the glove

matching the neck line, as indicated on the pattern. Make sure the top of the glove is unrestricted, then ladder stitch the head to the glove.

Ears Place one felt ear lining and one fur fabric ear piece together with the pile inside. Pin then backstitch the outside edges together, leaving the bottom straight edge open. Turn to the right side. Fold each corner of the straight edge into the centre of the ear and secure. Make the other ear in the same

way. Ladder stitch the ears to the head using the colour plate as a guide to correct placing. If you wish to protect the ears from being pressed flat by the box lid, glue a section cut from the kitchen towel roll to the inner centre of the box lid. The depth of the section is determined by the length of the ears. Cover the tube and its end with felt to match the lid (first covering the end with a circle of strong card). The ears then remain upright on either side of the tube, which pushes on the top of the head. This method requires a deeper box.

Tail Join the main body colour tail half to the white half of the pattern. Gather around the outside edge, pull up slightly and stuff, then pull up firmly and fasten off. Ladder stitch the tail to the back of the glove at the centre, approximately 7.6cm (3in) up from the hemmed bottom edge, with the main body colour of the tail uppermost.

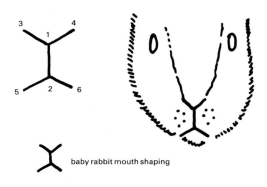

baby rabbit mouth shaping

Diagram 29 Mouth shaping: the numbering indicates the working order of stitching

Work the mouth and the nose using three strands of stranded embroidery silk.

Apply the whiskers on either side of the head between the nose and the mouth using the method outlined in Project 12.

Baby rabbit With the right sides facing, place the body side pieces together. Pin then backstitch from (c) at the neck to (a). Insert the head gusset (a–b), pin and backstitch into place. Backstitch the outside edges together from (b) to the stuffing opening. Insert the stomach gusset (c–d) and stitch into place; on the second side of the gusset continue joining the outside edges round to the stuffing opening. Turn to the right side.

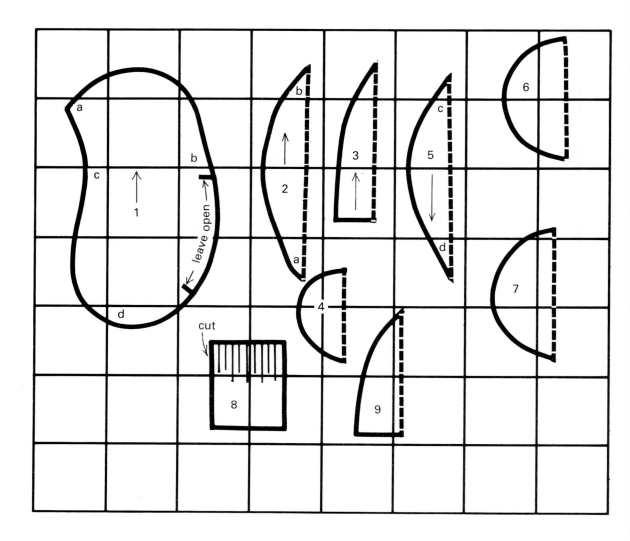

Baby rabbit pattern pieces

1 Body: cut two (one reversed) in short pile fur fabric.
2 Head gusset: cut one in short pile fur fabric.
3 Ears: cut two in fur fabric, cut two in felt.
4 Paws: cut two in fur fabric.
5 Stomach gusset: cut one in fur fabric.
6 Feet: cut two in fur fabric.
7 Tail: cut one in fur fabric.
8 Carrot top: cut one in light green felt.
9 Carrot: cut one in orange felt.

Insert the safety lock eyes. Stuff firmly and ladder stitch the opening to close. Construct the ears as for the adult rabbit and ladder stitch in place. Work the mouth and nose using two strands of stranded embroidery silk. Add two whiskers on either side of the nose.

Gather the paw circles and stuff to form small balls, then ladder stitch to the body on either side of the stomach gusset just under the neck. Treat the foot circles in the same way and ladder stitch to the body just under the paws. Gather and make the tail in the same way and ladder stitch to the body at the base of the back at the centre.

Carrot Fold in half and overstitch around the outside edge, leaving the top straight edge open. Stuff. Gather the top edge and close. Roll up the green felt carrot top and place a holding stitch. Ladder stitch over the gathered top of the carrot. Stitch the carrot to the baby rabbit's left paw. Ladder stitch the baby rabbit to the left arm of the rabbit glove.

Box Follow Method 2 in the previous book. Cover four of the side card panels and the lid with light green felt on the outside and dark brown felt on the inside, allowing a 0.7cm (¼in) felt excess all round each card piece. The felt should be stretched over the panels to produce a firm fit. Pin then stab stitch around the outside edges and fasten off. Trim the felt outside edges, leaving sufficient felt edge to enable the panels to be stitched together.

Cover the remaining two panels on one side only, one in light green felt and the other in dark brown felt. On the dark brown panel allow an extra 0.7cm (¼in) all round to turn under the card and glue into place. This inner covered card will be used later to secure the spring.

Construct the box by pinning the covered card panels together and overstitching the sides and the base firmly together.

Fitting the spring
Take the inner base piece of card which is covered with brown felt on one side only. Place the spring in an upright position in the centre of the card on the felt side. Insert the bottom coil of the spring about one turn under this inner base card. Glue the spring into place and add a few stitches to hold the spring securely to the card. If the card is very strong, then stitching will not be possible, so add adhesive tape to hold.

Cover the base of the spring to a depth of about 3.8cm (1½in) with a piece of cardboard tube cut from the inside of a disposable towel roll. Glue the base of the tube to the inner card lining base piece to hold it in place around the spring. Cover the outside of the tube with dark brown felt to match the lining. The placing of this tube guides the spring as the lid of the box is raised and contains it as the lid is lowered. Glue the inner base with the attached spring construction to the base of the box.

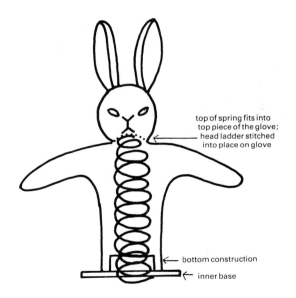

top of spring fits into top piece of the glove; head ladder stitched into place on glove

bottom construction

inner base

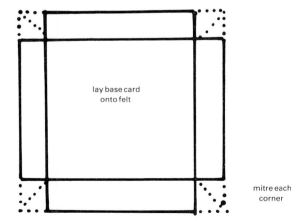

lay base card onto felt

mitre each corner

Diagram 30 Method of covering card with felt to form panels from which the box is constructed

Diagram 31 Spring construction

Place the glove over the spring. Glue the bottom hemmed edge of the glove to the inner base, then take stitches through the neck edge of the head to secure it to the spring.

An alternative way of adding the spring construction is to leave the base panel of the box open at the box construction stage, then the box base panel can be glued to the spring base and, when complete, can be inserted into the base of the box and stitched into place.

Applying the lid
Either oversew one edge of the lid to the back edge of the box or, if preferred, cut two felt hinges, sew one end of each to the lid and the other end to the back edge of the covered box.

Lid fastening
Decide on the method you prefer as listed under material quantities and apply to the box.

Trimming
Glue lampshade braid down the four corners of the box over the stitching, and turn the ends in neatly. Add various trimmings to simulate grass and flowers on the front and side panels of the box. The lid has a 5cm (2in) circle of yellow felt for the sun with yellow embroidery silk sun rays. A tree branch in brown felt is across one corner of the lid, with the branch design following down on to the front panel of the box, so that when the box is closed the branches on the lid and front marry up and look very effective. Lace flowers cut from trimming are glued on the branches. The colour plate shows all the panel decorations.

17
MATRIOCHKAS

SIZE
Height of the largest figure 17.8cm (7in)

GRADING
Moderately difficult

TECHNIQUES
Machine embroidery
Features using fabric paints

DESIGN BRIEF
A soft toy from a historical concept using machine embroidery

EVALUATION OF DESIGN BRIEF
The toy had to be a simple shape to permit the use of the machine embroidery: too complex a design would have detracted from the embroidery and made the felt figures difficult to insert into one another.

Figure 21. Matriochkas: mother, girl and baby

81

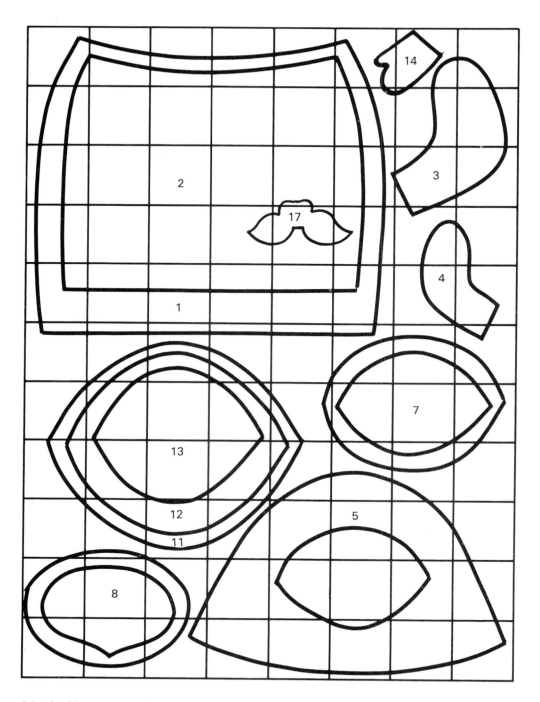

Matriochkas pattern pieces

1 Mother's body: cut two in orange Furmofelt.
2 Girl's body: cut two in green Furmofelt.
3 Mother's arms: cut two in green Furmofelt.
4 Girl's arms: cut two in red Furmofelt.

5 Mother's head: cut two in red Furmofelt.
6 Girl's head: cut two in orange Furmofelt.
7 Mother's face: cut one in flesh Furmofelt.
8 Girl's face: cut one in flesh Furmofelt.

DEVELOPMENT OF DESIGN

The first sketches of the toy at the design stage were of the traditional wooden nesting dolls with the shaped head and body. These proved a problem as a base for the embroidery, and also for stacking within each other as a soft concept, so the outline shape had to be simplified. This was not successful at first as it did not seem to relate to the original wooden dolls.

It would have been easy at this stage to discard the designs, and this rather proves that toymakers should not be too hasty in destroying their work, because, as more of the shapes were made to add to the family of nesting dolls, the more successful the design became.

CHOICE OF MATERIALS

Furmofelt was used, as this has a firm texture and will stand without wrinkling. It is flexible enough to withstand each subject being inserted into the other. (The address of the stockist is given at the end of this book.) If an alternative material is required, use Vilene Funfelt or ordinary felt and then attach iron-on Vilene to one side of the felt to stiffen it.

The amount and variety of the machine embroidery on the dolls is determined by the sewing machine available. Hand embroidery can be used as an alternative, and, whilst more time-consuming, can be very effective, especially if a variety of different thread types is used, for example fancy Lurex. To enable the reader to have complete freedom of design for their matriochkas, the actual type of stitches used on the photographed dolls is not given.

MATERIALS REQUIRED

The mother

Body
Orange Furmofelt 15.3cm (6in) × 12.7cm (5in)

Head
Red Furmofelt 14cm (5½in) × 17.8cm (7in)

Arms
Green Furmofelt 7.6cm (3in) × 10.3cm (4in)

The girl

Body
Green Furmofelt 12.7cm (5in) × 20.4cm (8in)

Head
Orange Furmofelt 11.5cm (4½in) × 14cm (5½in)

Arms
Red Furmofelt 6.4cm (2½in) × 5cm (2in)

The baby White Furmofelt 28cm (11in) × 12.7cm (5in)

Faces and hands for the three figures combined, flesh Furmofelt 14cm (5½in) × 10.3cm (4in)
Toy filling
Copydex
Fabric paints or felt painting pens
Pieces of coloured card for the two larger figure bases

CONSTRUCTION

Cut out all the pattern pieces as listed.

The mother Decorate the front and the back body pieces using a variety of embroidery stitches. The original model had a band of contrasting Furmofelt added 2.5cm (1in) up from the bottom edge, which gives extra support to the figure when it is finally assembled. Stitch a hand to each sleeve at the straight ends, and embroider the sleeves. Attach to the body using the photograph as a guide to placing.

The wooden matriochkas were usually painted in elaborate designs in a variety of colours, so use contrasting stitching in a range of colour tones to add interest to these felt figures. Add a 2.5cm (1in) strip of Furmofelt to the inside top of each body piece; this will give extra support to the figure when in use. Overstitch the side seams together on either side of the body, leaving the base and top open. Cut a piece of coloured card to the shape of the base, slightly smaller all round than the base size; glue to the felt base. Overstitch the base into the bottom of the body.

Head
Lay the front body piece on top of the face piece, and machine stitch around the outside edge using a fancy stitch. Paint on the features. Add the small flat bow just below the chin at the centre front.

Work a line of embroidery 0.7cm (¼in) up from the bottom edge, all round both head pieces. With wrong sides facing, overstitch the outside curved edges together leaving the bottom edge open.

The girl Make in the same way as the large figure.

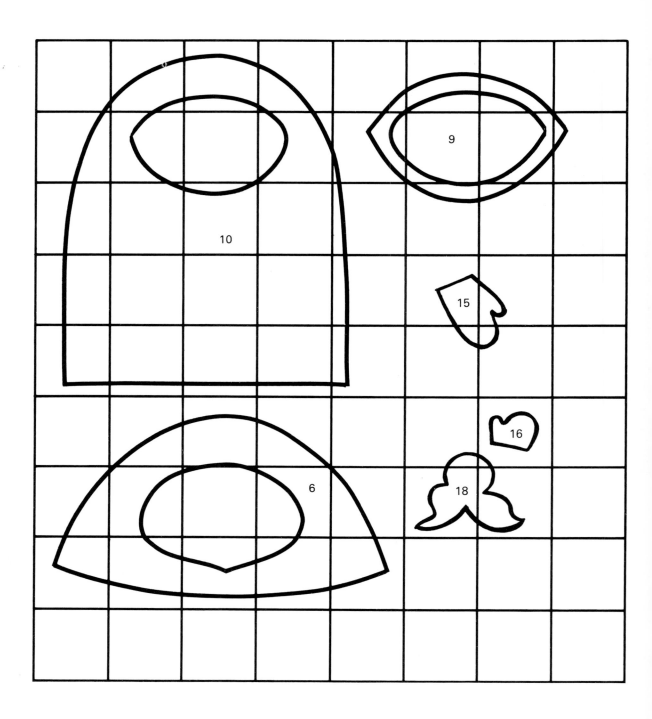

9 Baby's face: cut one in flesh Furmofelt.
10 Baby's body: cut two in white felt.
11 Mother's base: cut one in orange felt.
12 Girl's base: cut one in green felt.
13 Baby's base: cut one in white felt.

14 Mother's hands: cut two in flesh Furmofelt.
15 Girl's hands: cut two in flesh Furmofelt.
16 Baby's hands: cut two in flesh Furmofelt.
17 Mother's bow: cut one in red Furmofelt.
18 Girl's bow: cut one in orange Furmofelt.

Figure 22. Matriochkas: heads removed; baby inside
main body

Baby Place the front body piece over the face piece and stitch together. Add the features. Decorate around both body pieces with pale pink and green embroidery, so that when the body pieces are placed together at the construction stage the embroidery matches up. Place the body pieces together with the wrong sides facing, and overstitch the outside edges together, leaving the bottom edge open.

Cut a small slit to the size of the wrist 2.5cm (1in) down from the face on the right-hand side of the front body piece and 2.5cm (1in) in from the right-hand side seam. Insert the hand facing upwards towards the face. Insert the base into the bottom of the body leaving a small opening. Stuff and close the opening.

Matriochkas features (full size)

a Larger doll
b Medium size doll
c Baby doll

85

18
WIRED BABY DOLL

SIZE
Height 35.5cm (14in)

GRADING
Moderately difficult

TECHNIQUES
Wiring a toy. Laminating a doll mask

DESIGN BRIEF
A baby doll with a laminated face which can be manipulated into different positions

CHOICE OF MATERIALS
This doll is made in felt with a laminated face which can be likened to the Lenci dolls made by a similiar process. An alternative head pattern is supplied for those readers wishing to make a soft doll head, and this can be used as a basis for needle modelling or any other suitable technique. The wire armature

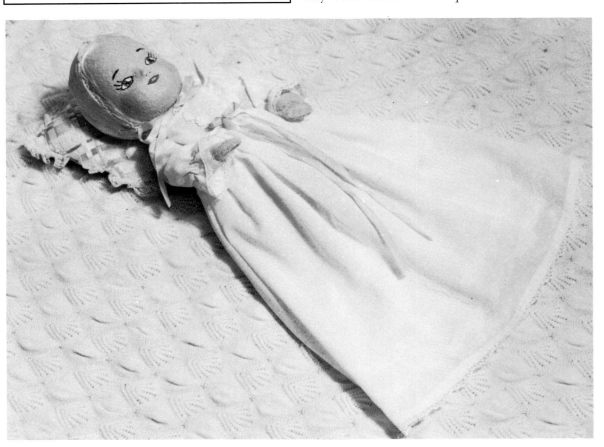

Figure 23. Wired baby doll

can be omitted if the doll is not required to be bendy: the soft head on a stuffed body being safer for a younger child.

MATERIALS REQUIRED

Body Flesh coloured felt measuring 40.6cm (16in) × 28cm (11in)

Laminated head Use either a doll mask measuring 17.8cm (7in) from the top of the head to the neck base, or a complete doll head in proportion to the body when made up. The laminating process is described in detail in the previous book with the materials required.

Soft head Flesh coloured felt measuring 30.5cm (12in) × 15.3cm (6in)

Wire for the armature Copper or galvanised wire about the size of a no. 12 or 13 (USA 1 or 0) knitting needle approximately 76.2cm (30in) long (the wiring process is described in the previous book)

Fabric paints
A doll wig or shaggy pile fur fabric
Toy filling
Flesh coloured sewing thread

CONSTRUCTION

Cut out the pattern pieces as listed.

Body Place the two pattern pieces together and neatly overstitch around the outside edge, leaving a stuffing opening at the neck and one shoulder, as indicated on the pattern. Lay to one side and prepare the wire armature.

Stuff the body at the feet and hands and lightly within the limbs and body, leaving room for the armature to be inserted. Carefully place the prepared armature into position within the body, taking care not to stretch the felt, and pack with toy filling until completely encasing it. The armature, if correctly covered at the preparation stage, should not be felt at all through the felt doll skin. Close the stuffing opening by overstitching to match the previously stitched body outline.

The doll's body is then needle modelled where indicated on the pattern, i.e. at the feet, knees, hands, wrists and elbows. To produce a more realistic shaping to the feet, after needle modelling, ladder stitch across each foot approximately 2.5cm (1in) up from the toe to the leg; this will turn each

foot upwards and also give shaping to the ankle. If this is not done, the feet can still be turned upwards by the wiring, but a bulge may form in the leg felt which could spoil the appearance of the doll.

Laminated head Prepare the laminated head. Stuff very firmly to support the mask shape and to prevent denting. A pattern is given in the graph for the back of the head if a doll mask has been produced rather than a full laminated head. It may be necessary to adjust the size in proportion to the laminated mask. Apply the head back to the laminated mask as described under the laminating process. Overstitch the lower edge of the laminated mask to the body where indicated.

Make sure the head is firmly stuffed at the neck then finally attach the back of the head to the body with ladder stitching. If the whole head has been laminated, it is easier to overstitch all round the neck edge on the head to secure to the body.

Soft head Insert the head gusset piece no. 3 between two of the no. 2 head pieces, and overstitch on both of the long edges to the head pieces where indicated on the pattern. Stuff the head. Needle modelling, contouring, embroidery and appliqué are all suitable techniques for producing the features and shaping. The extra no. 2 head piece is provided where it is necessary to hide any stitching on the back of the head which could result from some processes, for example needle modelling.

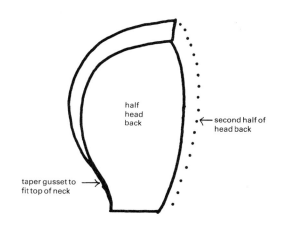

Diagram 32 Applying a back head piece to a laminated mask (a large head may require the addition of a gusset)

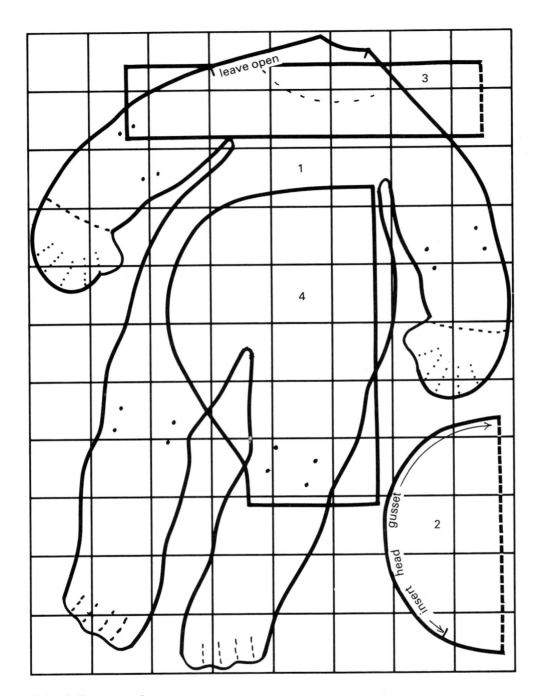

leave open

3

1

4

gusset

insert head

2

Baby doll pattern pieces

1 Body: cut two in felt.
2 Soft head: cut three in felt, i.e. one for the face and two
   for the head back. The extra piece is added after the
   needlemodelling is completed to hide the stitching.
3 The face head gusset: cut one, in matching felt.

4 Back of head for a laminated mask: cut two in felt. Join
   the long straight edges to the mask then stitch the back
   seams together, leaving the neck edge open. Stuff then
   ladder stitch to the body. For a fuller head add a
   straight gusset between the two head pieces (see
   Diagram 32).

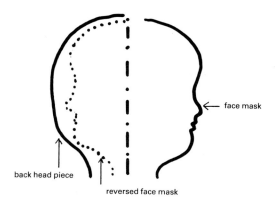

Diagram 33 Placing felt back head pieces on to a laminated face mask

After the shaping has been completed, the extra head piece is overstitched into place at the back of the head, to the previously stitched seam, and then stuffed to shape. The head is then ladder stitched to the body. It should be noted that, whichever head design is used, the top of the armature is inserted into the head and the toy filling is stuffed into the neck before the head is applied to the body.

Hair A doll wig can be used, although as this is a baby doll you may find most dolls' wigs are only suitable for older subjects. The baby doll in the photograph had blonde long pile fur fabric with the backing removed, glued to its head in locks.

Features For the laminated head the features are painted on with fabric paints copying the original doll mask or head. Avoid being too detailed, simplicity is the key to success. Do not use harsh colours.

BABY DOLL CLOTHES

A christening gown, bonnet and panties were designed for the wired baby doll

MATERIALS REQUIRED

60cm (24in) × 115cm (45in) material
1m (39in) narrow elastic
1½m (58½in) narrow ribbon
Oddments of Velcro or two snap fasteners

Lace The finished width of the skirt is 71.2cm (28in); multiply this by the number of rows of lace you wish to apply to the skirt.
Lace is also required for the sleeves, neck trimming and bonnet – approximately 1m (39in).

CONSTRUCTION

Panties Stitch the front and back seams and neaten. Stitch crutch seam and neaten. Fold top of panties to the fold line then over again to make a double hem, leaving a small gap to thread the elastic through. Do the same for the leg elastic but clip the lower edge first. Cut a piece of elastic to the doll's waist size plus 1.3cm (½in), thread through and stitch to fasten. Cut two pieces of elastic to the doll's leg size plus 1.3cm (½in), thread through each leg and stitch to fasten off.

Bonnet Stitch the darts. Stitch the head gusset to the bonnet sides matching the notches. Neaten the seams, and turn under a small hem at neck edge. Turn a small hem round the bonnet brim, then stitch narrow lace trimming round the brim. Cut two pieces of narrow ribbon each measuring 30.5cm (12in) long and stitch to the chin edge of the bonnet.

Dress Make a small double hem at the bottom edge of the sleeve; stitch then edge the hem with narrow lace. Gather the sleeve head between the notches. Clip the neck edge and turn under to the wrong side, then stitch lace to the neck edge. Fold the centre back to the fold lines and stitch. Pull up the gathers on the sleeve head to fit the armholes. Adjust the gathers. Stitch and neaten.

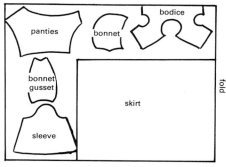

diagram of pattern layout for christening gown, bonnet and panties

Diagram 34 Pattern layout for christening gown, bonnet and panties (not to scale)

Make a small double hem along one long edge of the skirt piece; stitch and then attach lace as for the sleeve. Gather the other long edge for the waist. Pull up the gathers to fit the bodice, adjust, pin and stitch. Stitch the centre back seam leaving the seam open for approximately 10.3cm (4in) from the waist seam. Cut two pieces of narrow ribbon each measuring 43.7cm (17in) and fasten to the waist seams at the back; tie to form a bow at the centre

front. Sew snap fasteners or Velcro to fasten the back.

Trimming The trimming can be fun, either simple or very fussy, depending on the material being used. The christening gown on the photographed felt doll has two extra rows of ribbon added to the skirt and three small broderie anglaise daisies sewn on to the bodice.

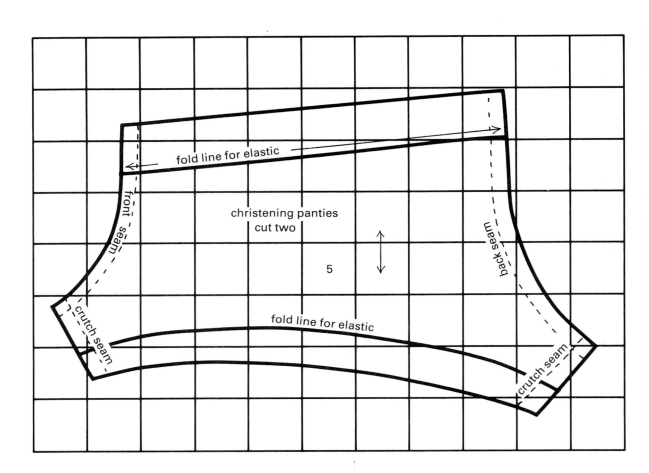

Clothes pattern pieces

Skirt: cut one on fold to measure 73.7cm (29in) × 35.5cm (14in).
1 Bodice: cut one.
2 Sleeves: cut two.
3 Bonnet: cut two.
4 Bonnet gusset: cut one.
5 Panties: cut two.

Top

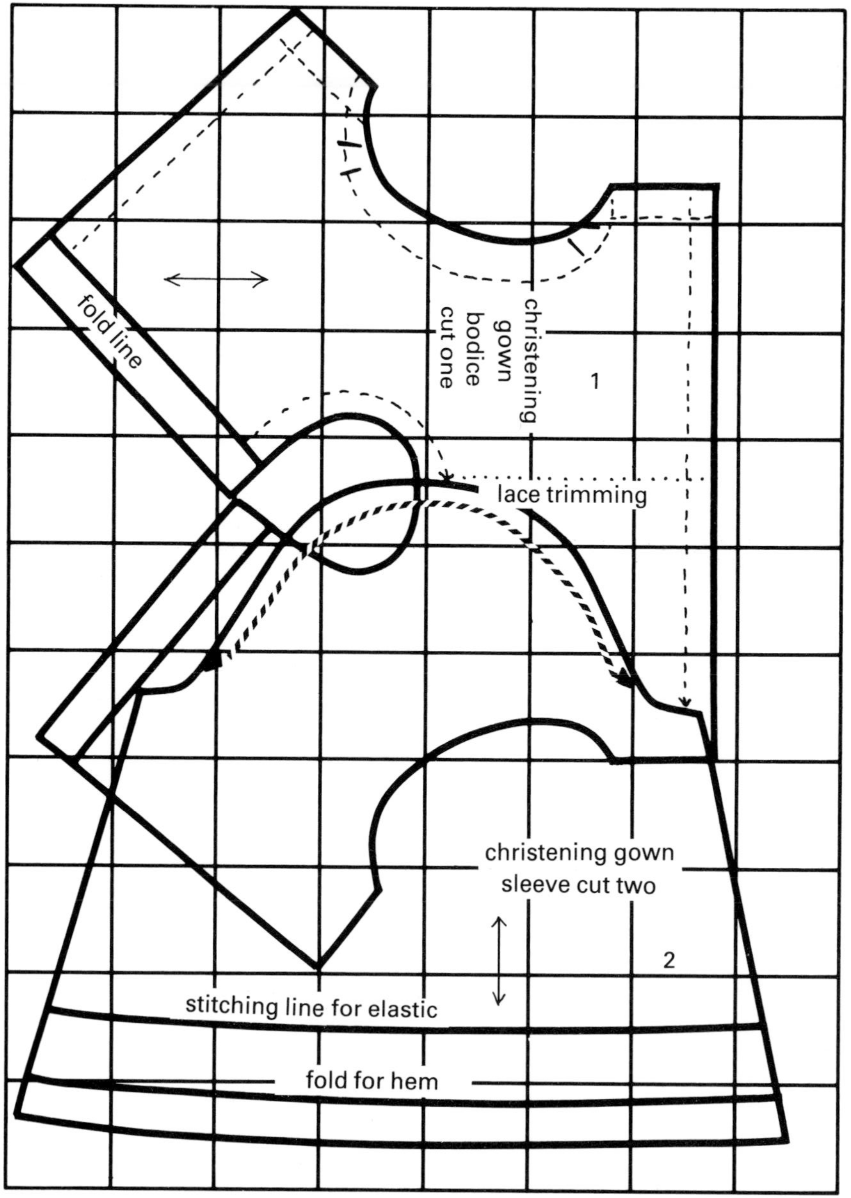
christening gown bodice cut one
1
fold line
lace trimming
christening gown sleeve cut two
2
stitching line for elastic
fold for hem

Top

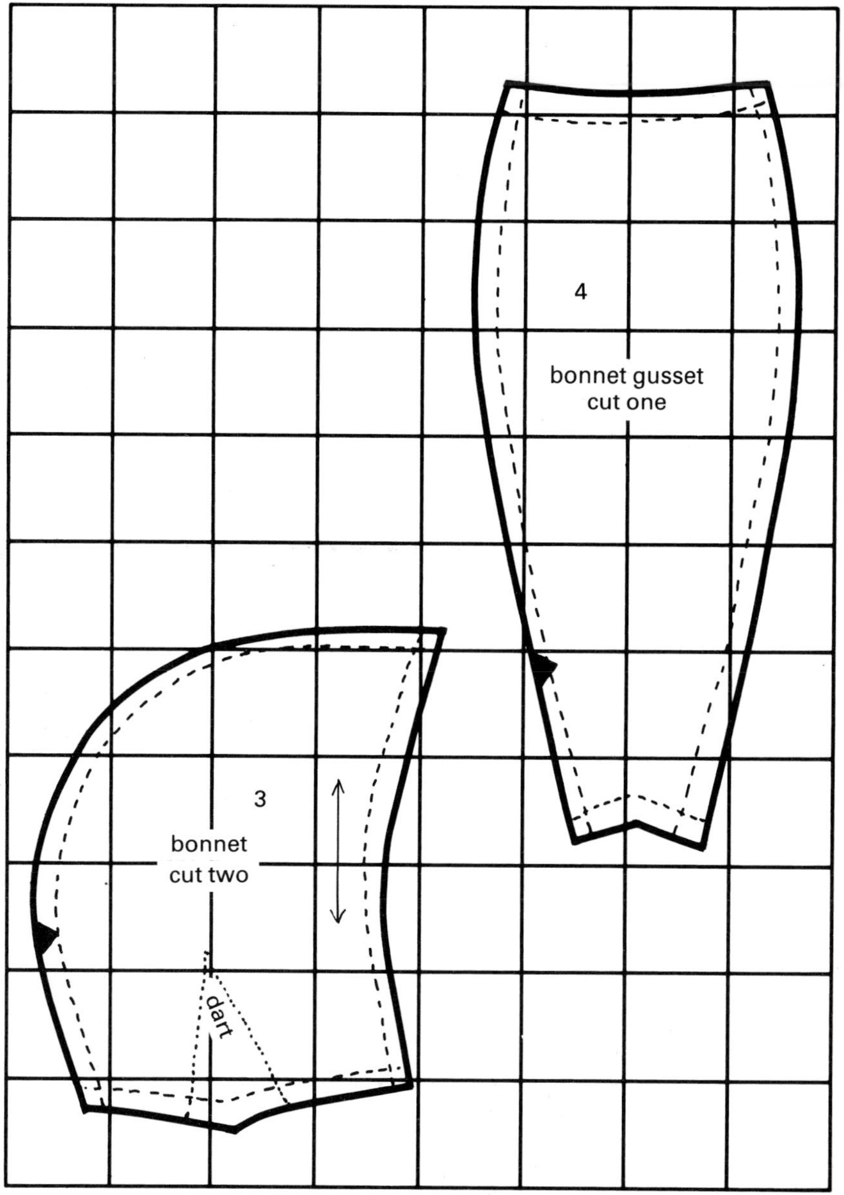
4
bonnet gusset cut one
3
bonnet cut two
dart

19
RABBIT STICK PUPPET

GRADING
Moderately difficult

TECHNIQUES
A wooden spoon-based puppet. Hat construction

DESIGN BRIEF
A soft toy stick puppet

EVALUATION OF DESIGN BRIEF
Conjurors produce a white rabbit out of a hat, so this was the theme adopted for this stick puppet. Ready-made hats can be obtained from a variety of sources and, if in a suitable style, can easily be adapted to accommodate this rabbit. The hat construction is given here for those toymakers who may not have a hat available in a suitable size and shape. Whether using a purchased hat or making a hat for this stick puppet, the main consideration is that the crown of the hat is large enough to contain the rabbit when it is hidden inside.

MATERIALS REQUIRED

The rabbit White short pile fur fabric 70.5cm (27¾in) × 24.8cm (9¾in)
White felt 14.6cm (5¾in) × 9cm (3½in)
One pair of 14mm blue safety lock eyes
Black stranded embroidery silk
Horsehair for the whiskers
Toy filling
One large wooden spoon

The hat Two 30.5cm (12in) diameter circles of black felt for the brim
Two pieces of black felt for the crown 58.4cm (23in) × 10.3cm (4in)
Two pieces of black felt for the top of the crown (the lid) 17.8cm (7in) diameter circles
Red lampshade braid 99.1cm (39in)
1m (39in) of 5cm (2in)wide black ribbon
Narrow black braid measuring 116.8cm (46in)
Card to the sizes of the black felt
Copydex or similar latex-based adhesive

CONSTRUCTION

The rabbit The complete rabbit glove is made in the same way as the jack-in-the-box rabbit, with the exception that the tail is made in half fur fabric and half white felt.

Insert the wooden spoon into the glove and push the bowl of the spoon into the top part of the glove which is inside the rabbit's head. Stitch around the neck of the rabbit and secure to just below the spoon bowl. Lay the prepared rabbit to one side.

Hat

Brim
Cut a 30.5cm (12in) diameter circle in the card. Glue the two same size circles of black felt to either side of the card, making sure that the felt is securely applied over all the surfaces. Trim around the outside edge with the red braid and glue to cover the felt and card joins.

Crown
Cut a piece of card measuring 55.9cm (22in) × 10.3cm (4in) and glue the two black felt pieces measuring 58.4cm (23in) × 10.3cm (4in) on either side of the card. Fold into a circle, the 2.5cm (1in) excess on the felt pieces overlapping – one on the inside of the crown and one on the outside. Glue together and, if necessary, add some stitching to hold. Glue the base of the crown to the brim, placing it centrally. Trim around the top edge of the crown with narrow black braid, gluing to hold in place.

Treat the top of the crown (lid) as for the brim, adding narrow black braid around the outside edge, but leaving 7.6cm (3in) free from the braid at the back. Use this to stitch the felt on the top of the crown (lid) to the top of the crown to make a hinge.

Hatband

Measure around the base of the crown and cut a piece of black ribbon to fit. Place around the crown and stitch the ends together at one side of the hat. Cut a 31.7cm (12½in) length of the black ribbon and lay it on a flat surface. Pick up the ribbon on either side of the centre and fold each end inwards slightly until the folds measure 9cm (3½in) across; stitch to hold. Take a separate 7.6cm (3in) length of the ribbon and fold in half lengthways with the edges meeting at the back. Lay this folded ribbon across the centre of the previously folded ribbon and glue the ends at the back to hold. This forms a flat bow which is then glued over the joins on the hatband.

Inserting the puppet into the hat Make a hole in the centre of the hat brim – this should be parallel to the centre of the crown. Add glue to the hemmed edge of the rabbit glove. Insert the spoon handle into the crown hole and pull through under the brim. Press the glued hem edge on the glove to the inside base of the crown. Wooden spoons usually have a shaped end to the handle which adds a decorative finish to this toy.

To prevent the spoon handle disappearing into the hat from under the brim when used by an over-enthusiastic presenter, or if the hole becomes bigger with wear, it is a simple matter to cut a strong card circle to the diameter of the top of the spoon handle. Then cut the circle open, insert it over the spoon handle and push it up until it is under the hole; glue to attach and close to the underbrim. Make a hole in the end of the spoon handle, thread a piece of cord through and tie in a knot.

The rabbit folds into the hat when the end of the spoon is pulled down under the brim, and it pops out of the crown when the wooden handle is pushed upwards. As the spoon bowl is secured inside the puppet's head, this achieves the maximum of manipulation and enables the spoon handle to be twisted, thus turning the puppet from side to side.

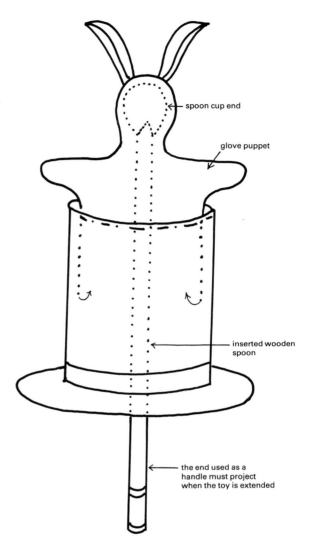

Diagram 35   Rabbit stick puppet construction

93

20
DOUBLE-EXPRESSION RAG DOLL

Figure 24. Double-expression rag doll: asleep features, nightdress and mob cap

SIZE
Height 53.3cm (21in)

GRADING
Difficult

TECHNIQUES
Embroidered features; reversable head technique; stitched hinging; sawdust and glue filled feet, and dressing a toy

DESIGN BRIEF
An original dressed rag doll using various toymaking techniques

EVALUATION OF DESIGN BRIEF
There are many rag doll patterns and countless examples seen in craft shops. When faced with the task of designing yet another rag doll, it becomes very difficult to be original. A technical approach can be an exciting challenge, and visits to various museums can sometimes produce ideas on which to base a design. This doll pattern is a soft version based on the early German dolls which had a china or composition head on top of which was a knob to turn the head from back to front with a different expression: awake/asleep, sad/happy and so forth.

DESCRIPTION OF THE DESIGN
The head comprises four sections which balance perfectly on the disc joint neck. The prototype of this doll was tested over a long period to show any weak areas in design. The knob construction is based on the method described in the previous volume, with slight alterations.

A dressed rag doll can look very floppy if stitch hinged at the elbows and below the shoulder, which can spoil the line of the clothes, and, as this rag doll was to be more sophisticated, stitch hinging was added below the shoulder to allow movement, and hinging was omitted on the curve of the arm to produce solidarity when the doll is wearing clothes. A new method of hinging was designed using a tape to take the constant strain on the arms when the child pulls on them to remove the clothes.

The legs were simply shaped and stuffed, with solid feet produced by sawdust and glue filling. The firm legs make it easier for the child to fit the pantaloons on the doll.

CHOICE OF MATERIALS

Rag dolls often choose their own materials! The toymaker may try several material types when suddenly the doll takes life with a particular material and that becomes the final choice. The rag doll pattern here required calico for the body – this will stand excessive wear and the texture complements the traditional approach.

A mixture of toy fillings was used, with terylene for the arms, body and legs. The feet had sawdust mixed with glue inserted, partly to add weight to the legs, the foot being the centre of gravity, and partly to make a firm foot for a child to fit the shoe on – much easier than a soft foot.

The shaped hands would have been nicer made in felt or cotton poplin material, but toymakers sometimes have to make a decision between what is most attractive for their creation and what is more practical for the use and wear of the toy. A toy is a toy and must last through endless play; a model is made to perfection in finer materials. There is a danger when designing a toy that the designer may become so motivated as the toy develops, that gradually the design brief criterion becomes less obvious and the end result could be a completely unsuitable design for the original requirement.

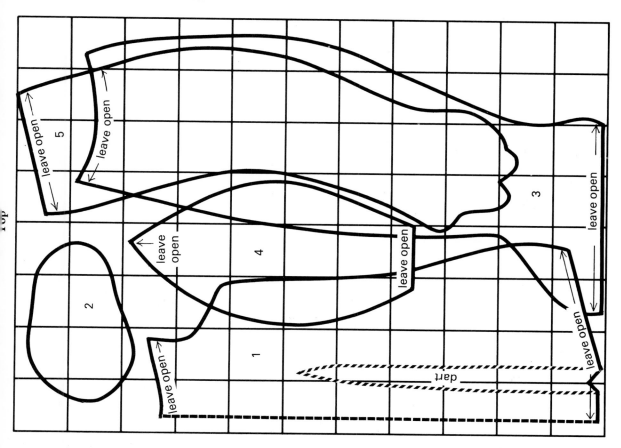

Rag doll pattern pieces

1 Body: cut two in calico. Dart on body where indicated.
2 Soles of feet: cut two in calico.
3 Legs: cut four in calico.
4 Head: cut four in calico.
5 Arms: cut four in calico.

Rag doll features (full size)

Eyebrows: single strand stitches. Brown.
Eyelids: single strand stitch. Cream.
Eyelashes: single strand stitches. Dark brown.
Corners inside eyes: peach.
Mouth: small backstitch. Peach.
Outline of eyes: peachy beige.
Eye pupils: black.
Highlights: white.
Mouth: peachy beige.
Nose: peachy beige.
Stitches radiating from the pupil: brown straight stitches.

Stranded embroidery threads are used for embroidering these features.

MATERIALS REQUIRED
Unbleached calico 64.8cm (25in) × 62.2cm (24½in)
Terylene toy filling
Sawdust or white sand
Wallpaper adhesive, Polycell or similar
1m (39in) of narrow cream lace
One brown doll wig or a ball of mohair yarn
Embroidery silks in brown, beige, pale pink, black and white
Lampshade braid 22.9cm (9in) (referred to as gimp) or, if not available, a strong thick tape
One 4.5cm (1¾in) hardboard joint set

CONSTRUCTION
Cut out all the pattern pieces as listed.

Head With the right sides facing, place the four head segments together and tack (baste) the seams together, leaving the top points and bottom straight edges open. Stitch together then turn to the right side.

Turning knob Bind a wooden clothes peg, the type without a spring, from just below the knob, and bind each prong separately, leaving the prong ends free from binding for 1.3cm (½in). Measure the length of your doll's head from the top to the neck edge, and make the length of the peg up to the same measurement by adding a small block of wood approximately 2.5cm (1in) × 4.5cm (1¾in). Insert each prong into the wood by cutting half circles to accommodate the slightly shaped ends of the peg, and leaving a bar across the centre to the width of the distance apart of the prongs (see Figure 28). Glue the prongs in place using a woodworking adhesive such as Evostick.

Joints Cut two circles of calico larger all round than the joint size and gather to cover the smooth inside of each joint half; pull up tightly and fasten off. Place the cotter pin through one half of the joint with the ends extending through the covered side of the joint. Glue the bottom of the block of wood to the disc. It will be necessary to cut a small indentation in the underneath of the block of wood to cater for the top of the cotter pin, prior to gluing the block and disc half together.

Partially stuff the head and insert the prepared knob, making a channel through the toy filling, until the knob at the top of the head protrudes above the points on the head segments. Fold in each top point at (a) on each head segment and add more

Double-expression rag doll:
awake features

Wired baby doll in christening outfit

Rabbit stick puppet

filling to the head; stitch the folds together surrounding the knob. Stuff the head firmly prior to turning in the neck edge and overstitching round the outside of the covered joint. Make sure, before completely closing, that the neck is well stuffed.

Body Dart the body where indicated. Place the body pieces together and, with the right sides facing, join the outside edges leaving the neck and bottom edge open. Turn to the right side.

Insert the second half of the disc joint into the neck edge with the material covering on the disc joint uppermost, by turning the neck edge in slightly and overstitching to the outside edge of the joint.

Insert the cotter pin protruding from the head joint into the second joint half, add the second washer, then pull and bend the cotter pin to secure the joint halves together (see disc jointing in the previous book).

Arms With the right sides facing, place the arm pieces together in pairs and stitch around the outside edges to join, leaving the top edge of each arm open. Turn to the right side. Stuff to within 6.4cm (2½in) of the top of each arm, and stitch across the arm at an angle as shown at c–d on the diagram. This section is left free of filling, and will assist the mobility of the arm.

Take a 22.9cm (9in) piece of flat lampshade braid (gimp) or very strong tape and cover with calico which has previously been stitched into a tube to the same length and width. Insert one end of the covered braid into the top of one arm for approximately 5cm (2in) and secure to the underarm. Turn in the top edge of the arm and gather to measure 3.8cm (1½in) across; add toy filling then press flat on to the tape and stitch the tape to the centre of the gathering.

Cut a small slit in the side of the body at shoulder level and insert the end of the tape into the shoulder,

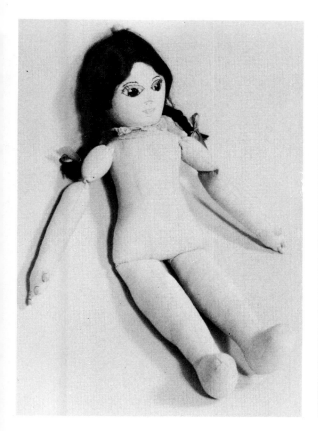

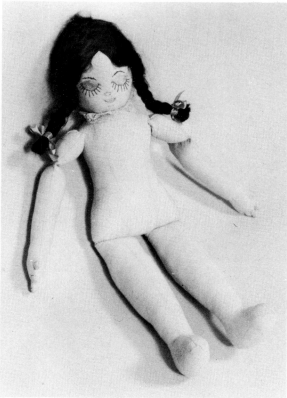

Figure 25. Double-expression rag doll: awake features, undressed

Figure 26. Double-expression rag doll: asleep features, undressed

97

pulling until the top of the arm meets the shoulder. Take the tape out through the slit and insert into the second arm in the same way as for the first. Turn in both sides of the body slits and stitch to the tape. Attach the gathered top of each arm to the shoulders on either side of the body by overstitching.

Stuff the body firmly, making sure that the shoulders are well stuffed, without impeding the line of the tape. Ladder stitch the base of the body together to close.

Hands Top stitch where indicated on the diagram to form the fingers and thumbs.

Legs With the right sides facing, place the leg pieces together in pairs; stitch the outside edges together leaving the top and bottom edges open. Insert a sole into the base of each leg. Turn to the right side.

Mix some sawdust with wallpaper adhesive, moisten it sufficiently to bind the sawdust together and insert it into the base of each foot to a depth of approximately 2.5cm (1in). If sawdust is not available, use silver sand with the adhesive. Leave to dry and then stuff the rest of the legs with terylene toy filling.

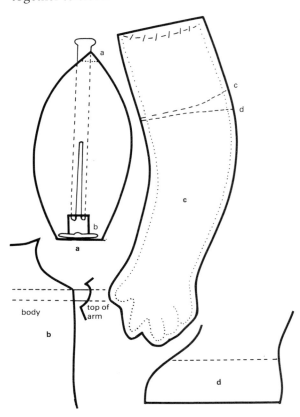

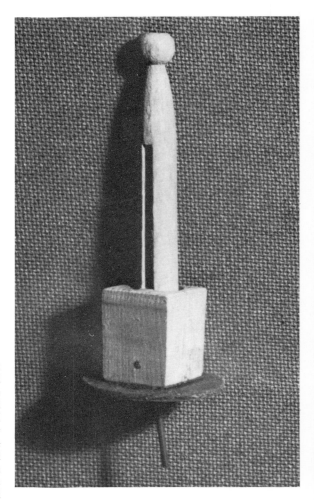

Diagram 36   a) Head construction: at (a) the top point on each head segment is folded inside the stuffed head and then stitched surrounding the protruding knob at the top of the head. The broken line indicates the peg placed inside the head and fixed into a small block of wood which is then glued to the head disc joint at (b). **b)** Body showing the insertion of the covered tape to apply the arm. **c)** Arm: the dotted line indicates stitching around the arm and to form the fingers; the broken line to (c–d) is top stitched after stuffing the lower arm. **d)** The foot is reinforced with sawdust or sand mixed with glue and inserted from the foot base to the broken line on the diagram.

Figure 27.   Double-expression rag doll: turning knob construction

If preferred, the feet can be stuffed with toy filling in the normal way. With the front seam at the centre, turn in the top edge on one leg and gather slightly. Place a holding stitch, then lay the front seam in line with the back seam and overstitch across the leg to attach to the body base seam, starting at the side of the body. Stitch the back of the leg also.

Treat the other leg in the same way, leaving a space of approximately 1.34cm (½in) between the top of the legs.

Neck trimming Cut a 0.5m (19½in) length of fine narrow cream lace and gather along one edge; pull up to fit the top of the body at the neck edge and stitch in place all round the neck. Treat the neck edge on the head in the same way. The lace trimming will mask the overstitching around the

disc edges and adds an attractive frill around the neck edges on day or underclothes; make sure, however, that the lace in no way impedes the disc movement.

Hair Pin the wig, or mohair yarn, into place on the centre of the head from side to side, leaving the front and back faces of the doll clear. Lightly draw the features on both faces with a pencil and embroider (see Diagram 37 for method of working). When the features are completed, check that the wig placing is correct in relation to the features, then stitch into place. The original doll has plaits, but many different hairstyles which could be adapted are given in the previous volume.

Figure 28. Double-expression rag doll: top view of base for turning knob construction

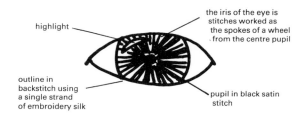

highlight

the iris of the eye is stitches worked as the spokes of a wheel from the centre pupil

outline in backstitch using a single strand of embroidery silk

pupil in black satin stitch

Diagram 37 Embroidering an eye

CLOTHES FOR THE DOUBLE-EXPRESSION RAG DOLL

MATERIAL QUANTITIES

Pantaloons and petticoat 50 cm (20in) × 90cm (36in) material
1.5m (1⅝yd) of pre-gathered broderie anglaise, or 3m (3¼yd) of 5cm (2in) wide lace (to be gathered)

Apron 25cm (10in) × 90cm (36in) material

Bonnet 35cm (14in) × 90cm (36in) material
Piece of interfacing measuring 35.5cm (14in) × 10.3cm (4in)

Dress 70cm (28in) × 90cm (36in) material
70cm (28in) of bias binding
20cm (8in) of pre-gathered broderie anglaise
25cm (10in) of narrow elastic
50cm (20in) of narrow ribbon
Two snap fasteners

Nightdress and mob cap 90cm (36in) of 0.7cm (¼in) wide lace
1.2m (1⅓yd) of 2cm (¾in) wide lace
90cm (36in) of 0.7cm (¼in) wide lace
50cm (20in) of narrow elastic
Two snap fasteners
60cm (24in) of bias binding

Boots Felt to tone with the dress material 22.9cm (9in) × 26.1cm (10¼in)
Six small buttons with shanks

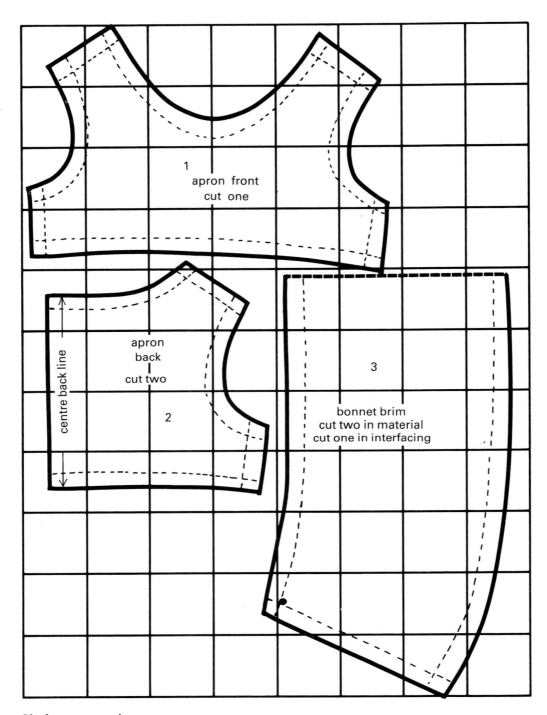

Clothes pattern pieces

1 Apron front: cut one.
2 Apron back: cut two.
3 Bonnet brim: cut two in material, one in interfacing.

100

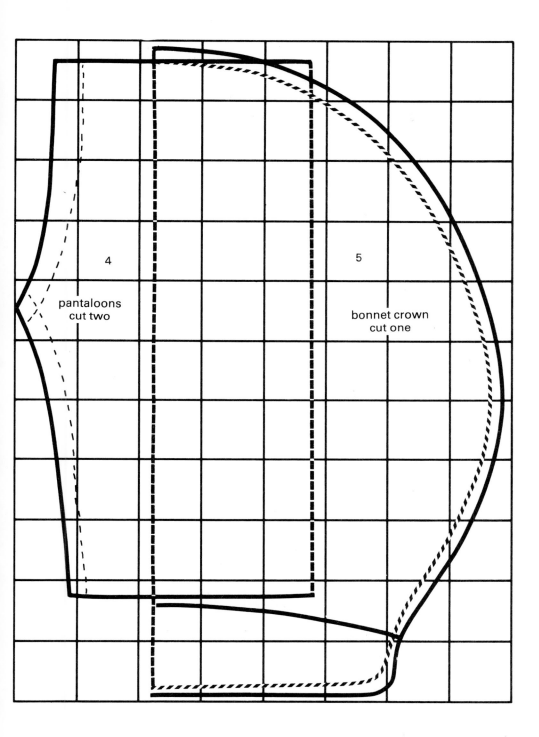

4   Pantaloons: cut two.
5   Bonnet crown: cut one.

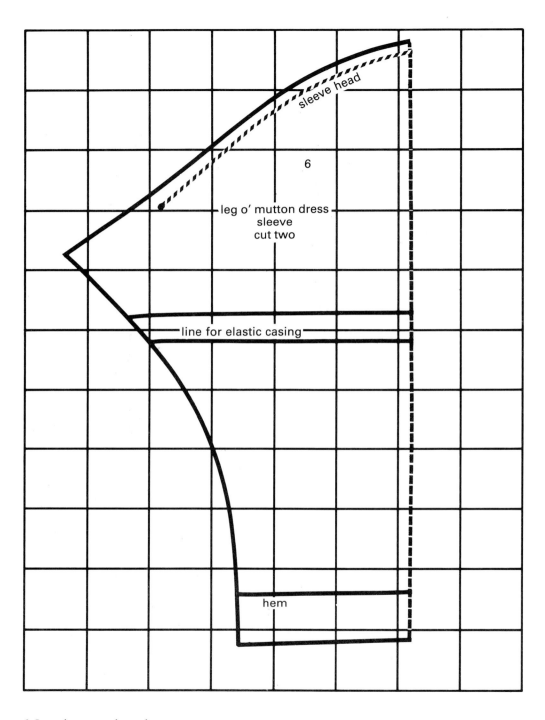

sleeve head

6

leg o' mutton dress
sleeve
cut two

line for elastic casing

hem

6 Leg o' mutton dress sleeve: cut two.

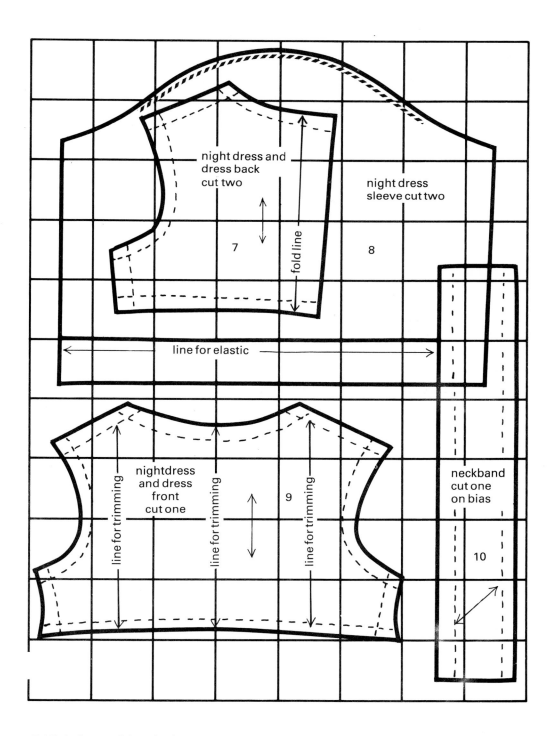

night dress and
dress back
cut two

fold line

7

night dress
sleeve cut two

8

line for elastic

nightdress
and dress
front
cut one

line for trimming

line for trimming

9

line for trimming

neckband
cut one
on bias

10

7 Nightdress and dress back: cut two.
8 Nightdress sleeve: cut two.
9 Nightdress and dress front: cut one.
10 Neckband: cut one on bias.

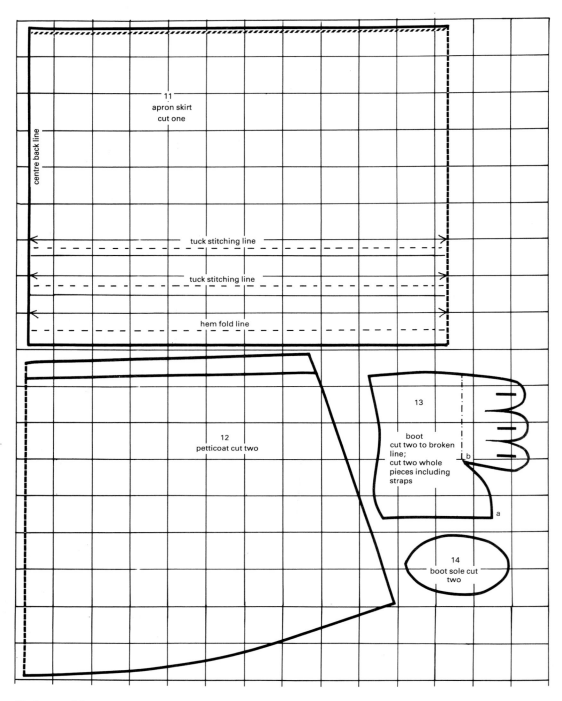

11 Apron skirt: cut one.
12 Petticoat: cut two.
13 Boots: cut two pieces to broken line; cut two whole pieces including straps in felt.
14 Boot sole: cut two in felt.

CONSTRUCTION

Dress Cut out all the pattern pieces as listed.

Bodice

Join the shoulder seams and neaten. With the right side facing, turn the fold line over to the wrong side and stitch. To neaten the neck edge, turn the raw edge to the wrong side and stitch.

Leg o' mutton sleeve

Stitch bias binding to line on the sleeve and thread approximately 12.7cm (5in) of narrow elastic through, stitching the ends to secure. Gather the sleeve head between the dots where indicated on the pattern and pull up to fit the bodice armhole. With the right sides of the bodice and sleeve facing, attach the sleeve to the bodice, adjusting the gathers. Make a small hem on the bottom of the sleeve. Join the side and sleeve seams.

Skirt

Cut a piece of material 91.5cm (36in) × 33cm (13in). Join the short seam for 17.8cm (7in), neaten and press the seam open. Run a gathering thread round the top of the skirt, and make a small hem the

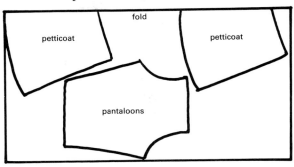

diagram of pattern layout for pantaloons and petticoat

Diagram 40 Pattern layout for pantaloons and petticoat (not to scale)

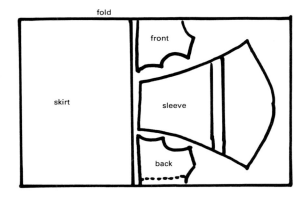

Diagram 38 Pattern layout for dress (not to scale)

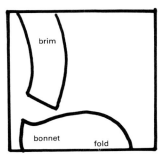

Diagram 41 Pattern layout for bonnet (not to scale)

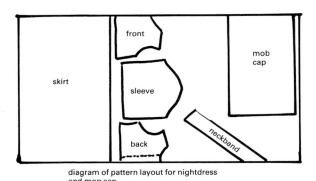

diagram of pattern layout for nightdress and mop cap

Diagram 39 Pattern layout for nightdress and mob cap (not to scale)

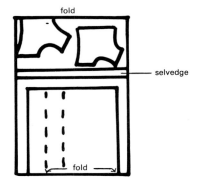

Diagram 42 Pattern layout for apron (not to scale)

other end. With the right sides together, join the bodice to the skirt, adjusting the gathers.

Finishing
To neaten the neck, apply pre-gathered broderie anglaise and a small bow at the centre front. Sew press studs to the back of the bodice.

Nightdress Cut out all the pattern pieces as listed. Make the bodice as the dress but neaten the neck with bias binding.

Sleeve
Make a small hem on the bottom of the sleeve and apply narrow lace 1.3cm (½in) from the hem. Stretch and apply a piece of elastic – this will make the cuff. Treat the other sleeve in the same way and continue making instructions as for the dress; stitch 2.5cm (1in) wide lace round the skirt hem.

Mob cap Cut a piece of material 63.5cm (25in) × 24.1cm (9½in). Stitch the short seam to make a tube. Along one long edge, turn up 3.8cm (1½in), and turn a 0.7cm (¼in) seam to the wrong side. Stitch, leaving a 0.7cm (¼in) gap through which to thread the elastic, then stitch again, 1.3cm (½in) from the first stitching. Stitch 2.5cm (1in) wide lace round the bottom hem.

Turn under a small hem on the unfinished edge of the tube. Run a gathering thread round the top and pull up tight. Thread elastic through the casing to fit the doll's head.

Pantaloons Stitch the crutch seams together and neaten. Turn the top over to the fold line; turn under a small hem and stitch round, leaving a small gap through which to thread the elastic. Turn up a small hem on the lower edges, attaching lace or broderie anglaise trimming at the same time. Stitch the inner leg seam and neaten. Thread elastic through the waist to fit the doll.

Petticoat Join the side seams and neaten. Make a casing for elastic as for the pantaloons. Turn up a small hem on the lower edge, attaching lace as before (a pre-gathered broderie anglaise looks pretty). Thread elastic through the waist to fit the doll.

Bonnet Gather around the long edge of the crown between the dots. Clip to the dots. Stitch under 0.7cm (¼in) on the lower edge between the dots.

Gather along the solid line, then just above the solid line, and pull up to measure 10.9cm (4¼in). Turn under 0.7cm (¼in) on the notched edge of one brim piece, then place two pieces of brim together and put interfacing underneath. Stitch between the dots, leaving the notched edge open. Clip the curves. Turn right side out and press.

With the right sides together, pin the crown to one brim section, matching the small dots; pull up the gathers evenly. Stitch, being careful not to catch in the turned edge of the brim. Slip stitch the turned in edge of the brim over the seam.

Apron Stitch the bodice front to the back at the shoulder seams. Stitch under 0.7cm (¼in) on the armhole and neck edges, clipping the curves. If you have a zigzag stitch on your sewing machine, this makes a neat and pretty finish. Stitch the side seams. Make tucks on the skirt where indicated on the pattern. Make the hem as for the armhole and neck, and gather the skirt where indicated between the large dots. Join the skirt to the bodice, adjusting the gathers. Turn the centre back to the fold line and neaten. Finish with two press studs.

Boots Place the boot pieces together in pairs comprising one small and one strapped piece. Join the back seams together and the front seams on the boot from (a) to (b). Turn inside out and stab stitch a sole into the base of the boot.

Place the boot on to a foot and fold the tabs across the leg until a firm fit is achieved. Mark where the buttons should be. Remove the boot and stitch the buttons in place. Buttonhole around the slits in the tabs. Treat the other boot in the same way.

Make sure as you make each boot that you place the piece with the tabs so that the tabs will face to the outside of each leg.

SIZE
Height 30.5cm (12in)

GRADING
Moderately difficult

TECHNIQUES
Disc jointing. Pad and paw application

DESIGN BRIEF
A lightweight disc jointed bear, not too large so that it is easy for the child to handle

EVALUATION OF DESIGN BRIEF
The teddy bear has been a successful and long-lasting character in the world of soft toys, and it would seem that a book on soft toymaking would be incomplete without a bear pattern. The pattern included here was one that I have been using for 29 years, originally making it when at school. Earlier the limbs were applied using ladder stitching but over the years it became altered eventually to being disc jointed. The nun who taught me my first toymaking gave us the pattern, and I have yet to find a more appealing design.

CHOICE OF MATERIALS
Most short pile fur fabrics are suitable for this toy. The colour chosen for this bear is the more traditional beige tone with matching felt paws and foot pads. Almost any colour tone is suitable. A contrast felt to the body fur fabric can look very effective – for example a white bear with pale blue felt paws and pads, using blue safety lock eyes and matching satin ribbon bow. Hardboard or wooden disc joints are the more satisfactory to use. The plastic safety lock type joints will not give the years of service required.

MATERIALS REQUIRED
Fur fabric – short pile fur fabric 46cm (18in) × 50.8cm (20in)
Felt for paws and pads 10.3cm (4in) × 10.3cm (4in)
One pair of 16mm safety lock eyes
One bear safety lock nose size 20mm
Toy filling
Stranded embroidery thread for claw and mouth marking
One disc joint for neck size 4.5cm (1¾in)
Two disc joints for arms size 3.3cm (1¼in)
Two disc joints for legs size 3.8cm (1½in)

Figure 29. Jointed teddy bear

It will be necessary to refer to the section 'Toys

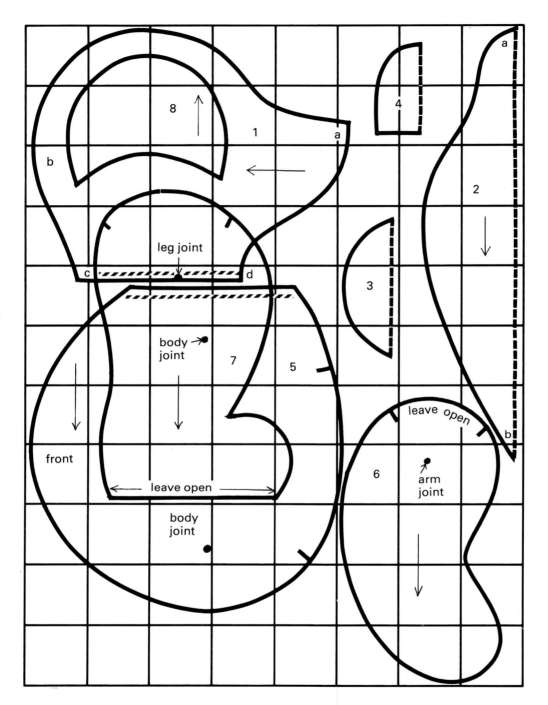

Teddy bear pattern pieces

1 Head: cut two in fur fabric (one reversed).
2 Head gusset: cut one in fur fabric.
3 Foot pads: cut two in felt or suede.

4 Paws: cut two in felt or suede.
5 Body: cut two in fur fabric (one reversed).
6 Arms: cut four in fur fabric (two reversed).
7 Legs: cut four in fur fabric (two reversed).
8 Ears: cut four in fur fabric (two reversed).

with Joints' in the previous book, and to prepare the joints as instructed.

CONSTRUCTION

Cut out the pattern pieces as listed.

Head Place the head pieces together and sew the muzzle seam (a-d). Insert the head gusset between the side head pieces matching (a-b) on gusset to (a-b) on the head pieces. Pin and then backstitch one side of the gusset at a time from (a) to (b). On the second side work from (a) to the base of the neck (c). Turn to right side.

Body With right sides together, pin then backstitch the centre front and centre back seam, leaving the opening in the back seam where indicated on the pattern, and the neck open also. Make sure you have stitched together the top back of the body from the neck edge to the back opening. Turn to the right side.

Arms Place the right sides together in pairs. Pin then backstitch around the outside edge, leaving the top of each arm open. Turn to the right side.

Legs Place the right sides together in pairs. Pin then backstitch around the outside edge, leaving the straight edge at the base of each leg open, and also the top of each leg open where indicated. Insert a foot pad into the base of each leg; pin and backstitch in place using a thread to match either the pad colouring or the skin fabric, whichever will be less noticeable. Turn to the right side.

Ears Place the right sides together in pairs, leaving the bottom edges open; pin then backstitch together. Turn to the right side. Overstitch each ear base separately and pull up to form a gentle curve; fasten the thread to hold.

Eyes and nose Lightly stuff the head temporarily to enable the correct marking of the eye position. It assists at this stage if the ears are pinned into place. A very common fault is that the eyes are inserted, the head is then stuffed which pushes the snout forwards, and the eyes often appear to be almost in the ears.

Remove the toy filling and insert first the safety lock nose and then the safety lock eyes where previously marked. Stuff the head firmly and gather the lower neck edge, inserting half of the neck joint. Pull up the neck edge and fasten off. Gather the neck edge on the body, pull up tightly and fasten off. Insert the second half of the neck joint in the top of the body. Secure the two joint halves together.

Stuff the limbs half way and joint each arm into the body and then each leg. Continue stuffing the arms until full and close the top opening on each using ladder stitching. Treat the legs in the same way.

Stuff the body firmly, taking particular care at the shoulders. Apply a pad on to each arm using ladder stitching. Take three strands of the embroidery thread and stitch claws on to each paw and foot pad. If required, embroider a mouth on the bear (see Diagram 45). Brush well with a teazle brush in the pile direction, paying particular attention to all the seams. Trim with a ribbon bow round the neck.

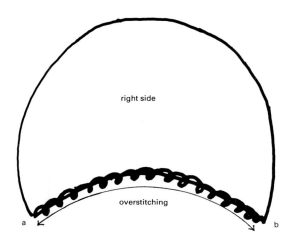

Diagram 43   Overstitching the base of a bear's ear

embroidered bear nose

Diagram 45   Embroidered bear nose. a) First stitch down towards the mouth shaping. b) Then stitch across from side to side.

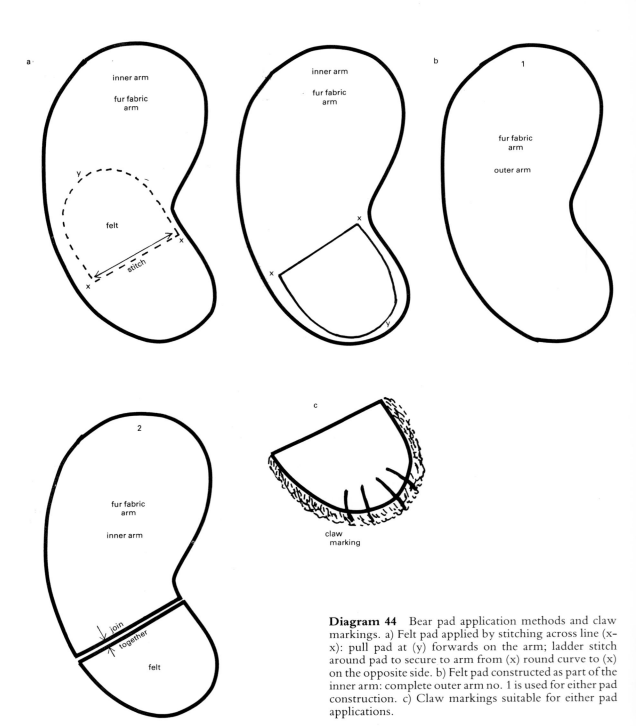

a

inner arm

fur fabric
arm

y

felt

x

stitch

x

inner arm

fur fabric
arm

x

x

y

b

1

fur fabric
arm

outer arm

2

fur fabric
arm

inner arm

join

together

felt

c

claw
marking

Diagram 44 Bear pad application methods and claw markings. a) Felt pad applied by stitching across line (x–x): pull pad at (y) forwards on the arm; ladder stitch around pad to secure to arm from (x) round curve to (x) on the opposite side. b) Felt pad constructed as part of the inner arm: complete outer arm no. 1 is used for either pad construction. c) Claw markings suitable for either pad applications.

GRADING
Moderately difficult

TECHNIQUES
Constructing a five piece pantin

DESIGN BRIEF
A pantin suitable as a soft toy image of the traditional wooden toy

EVALUATION OF DESIGN BRIEF
A pantin or jumping jack is usually made in thin plywood with brass screws and nuts, using cord with a wooden ball on the end for manipulating the pantin. The whole construction is then painted in non-toxic paint. There is a variation in the number of parts, but usually the construction comprises a body, arms, thighs and lower limbs, i.e. seven parts.

To adapt the traditional pantin to a toy with a soft appearance, strong card was used in place of wood, with fur fabric and felt applied to the front surfaces. The monkey pantin design was simplified in construction to five pieces, as the fur would have restricted the movement of the extra jointing. The original design comprised six pieces, which included a separate head.

If maximum joint movement is required in a fur fabric subject, it is necessary to leave the movable joints free from the fur fabric and often the card then shows which spoils the fur image.

The pantin construction given can be used as a basis for a variety of subjects. The design is flat so it is easy to cut out various subjects in their flat form.

MATERIALS REQUIRED
A piece of strong card 25.4cm (10in) × 35.5cm (14in) (oddments of card can be used according to the individual pattern piece requirement)

Four metal paper fasteners

Strong fine cord to manipulate the limbs, approximately 106.7cm (42in) for each arm and 76.2cm (30in) for each leg

Three beads approximately 0.7cm (¼in) in diameter (depending on the size of the hand of the child manipulating the toy, it may be necessary to have a larger bead for the manipulating thread)

A piece of fur fabric to cover the front of the pantin body and limbs 25.4cm (10in) × 35.5cm (14in)

A piece of felt for the face, hands and feet 8.3cm (3¼in) × 15.3cm (6in)

Oddments of fur fabric and felt can be used

One pair of 12mm safety lock eyes

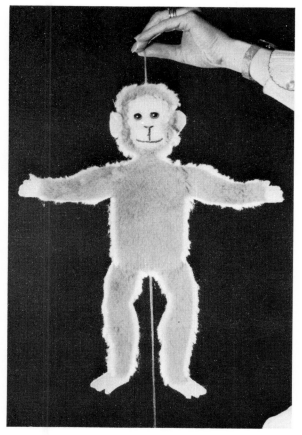

Figure 30.   Monkey pantin: front view

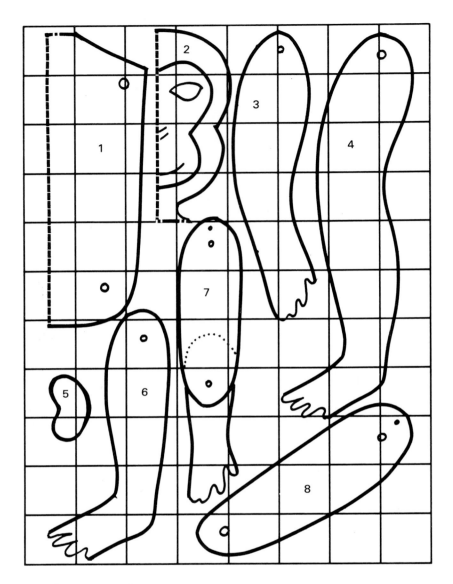

Monkey pattern pieces

Nos. 1, 2 (combined as one piece), 3, 4 and 5 are all that are necessary. The extra pattern pieces provided are to enable a larger construction pantin to be made for further subjects if required.

1 and 2 Make a combined head and body pattern. Cut one full pattern in fur fabric and one in card. Cut the monkey face in felt.

3 Non-jointed arm: cut two in fur fabric, cut two in card.

4 Non-jointed leg: cut two in fur fabric and two in card.

5 Ears: cut two in felt to match the face.

When making a pantin consisting of a larger number of pieces with jointed arms and legs, cut two lower leg pieces (No. 6) and two upper leg pieces (No. 8) in card, plus an extra piece for each in whatever material is being used as a covering. Each arm will require two pieces No. 7 upper and two pieces No. 7 lower arm, plus an extra piece for each in covering material.

If eyelids are required, cut a circle in felt to match the face, just larger than the eye and cut in half. Glue to secure around the top of each eye.

112

A small amount of toy filling
Stranded embroidery thread for marking the features
Copydex or similar latex-based adhesive
A small piece of adhesive tape for attaching the holding loop of cord to the top of the head.

CONSTRUCTION

Cut out pattern pieces nos. 1 and 2 combined, 3 and 4. Pattern pieces nos. 5, 6 and 7 are given to enable a six-piece jointed pantin to be made from further designs.

Pierce a small hole at the top of each arm and leg where indicated on the pattern. Pierce four holes in the body piece. Glue the felt hands and feet into place on the card limbs, matching up the shaping. Glue the fur fabric on to the limbs, making sure that the pile line is correct, i.e. from the top to the bottom of the pantin.

It should be noted when gluing the felt and fur fabric to the card that the adhesive will spread when pressure is put on it, and it is therefore advisable to apply the adhesive to within a short distance of the outside edge of the card pieces, then apply the fabric pieces and press outwards from the centre to the edge of each card. This will spread the adhesive to the edges rather than squeezing the surplus adhesive out of the edges and spoiling the fabric.

Starting with the arms, push a paper fastener from the front of the pantin through the card body piece and through the hole in the top of the fur-covered card arm. Press open the split ends of the fasteners to secure body and limbs together; treat the other arm in the same way. Do not pull the paper fasteners too tight or they will impede the movement.

If the fur fabric used has a fairly thick pile, it may be necessary, prior to applying the paper fastener, to trim off the pile at the top of the arm. Treat both legs in the same way. Trim the fur fabric as on the arms. Glue the fur fabric combined body and head piece on to the front of the card. This will mask the heads of the paper fasteners and make a good front surface for the limbs to work behind.

Insert the safety lock eyes into the felt mask piece and embroider the features. If the felt is rather thin, it may be necessary to back it with a lining, for example iron-on Vylene, prior to applying the eyes. Ladder stitch the face mask on to the fur fabric head piece, inserting some toy filling to shape it, prior to closing.

Study the monkey's expression and, if the eyes look too staring, which can happen with some

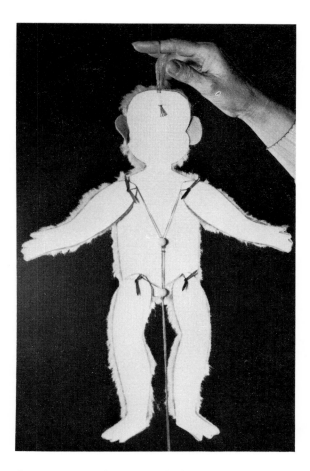

Figure 31.   Monkey pantin: back view

makes of eyes, glue an eyelid to the top of each eye, making sure the glue is used sparingly or it will spoil the shiny surface of the eyes. Ladder stitch the ears into place.

Take a piece of cord 17.8cm (7in) long, fold in half to form a hanging loop, and attach the two ends of the cord to the back of the head with adhesive tape approximately 2.5cm (1in) from the centre top of the head.

STRINGING THE PANTIN (see Diagram 46)

With the card backing uppermost, lay the pantin on to a flat surface. For each arm take a 106.7cm (42in) piece of cord. Fold it in half and, from the back of the arm, push the loop end through the hole at the top of the arm (a) to the card side of the arm. Take the end pieces through the loop of the cord and pull to tighten on to the curved top of the arm. Treat the other arm in the same way.

113

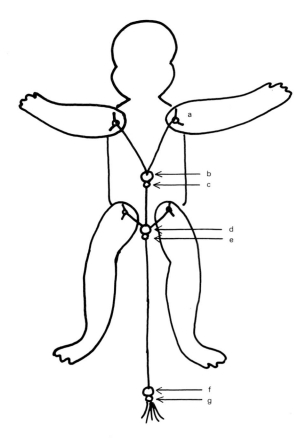

Diagram 46 Monkey pantin: back view showing string construction

upwards until the distance from the top bead to the second measures 5cm (2in) and the distance from the top of each leg cord to the second bead measures 5cm (2in) on each side. Make a knot under the second bead (e) and glue to hold the bead onto the top of the knot.

Take the eight cord ends together – they should measure approximately 35.5cm (14in) in length from the second bead. Thread these eight cords through the third bead (f), knot and glue the cord under this bead approximately 5cm (2in) up from the ends of the cord (g).

If preferred, after gluing the cord knot under the second bead below the legs, the eight cords can be plaited to within 5cm (2in) of the cord end and then have the third bead applied. This makes a strong manipulating cord. Depending on the thickness of card used for the pantin base, it is possible to make a very strong, heavier toy, in which case the manipulating cord would need to be correspondingly thicker and, instead of folding the limb cords in half, the cord would be single and knotted to the top of each limb. They would still be threaded through beads but ones of a much larger diameter.

When altering a design to make it heavier and more bulky, it is necessary to scale up everything accordingly.

To add fun, a felt banana can be attached to the monkey's paw.

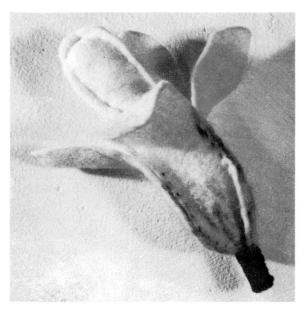

Figure 32. Banana for monkey pantin

Pull both of the arm cords taut at the centre of the body, approximately 17.8cm (7in) measured from the top of the head. Thread the four ends of the arm cords through a bead (b) and knot together under the bead (c). The distance from each arm top to the bead is approximately 7.6cm (3in). Add a small amount of adhesive to attach the bead on top of the knot. Lay these cords for the moment to the side of the body to avoid getting tangled with the next stage of stringing the legs.

Attach a 76.2cm (30in) piece of cord to the top of each leg by folding the cord in half and threading it as for the arms. Take hold of the four cords from the arms and thread these through a second bead (d), and thread the four ends from the tops of the legs through the same bead. Push the second bead

MATERIALS REQUIRED

Scraps of yellow and cream felt
Pieces of brown felt for the stalk
A brown felt-tipped pen
Small amount of toy filling

CONSTRUCTION

Using Diagram 47 as a guide, stab stitch the (a) pattern pieces together. Stuff firmly and close the opening. Top stitch the four pattern pieces (b) together half way up. Add a few stitches at the top of each section and pull up slightly to produce a curve. Insert the banana into the yellow skin and stitch to join with stab stitching.

Using the brown felt-tipped pen, mark lines down each ridge on the banana skin and draw lines of shading on the skin. Roll a small piece of brown felt tightly and stitch to hold the roll in place; ladder stitch the stalk to the banana skin (see completed banana on diagram).

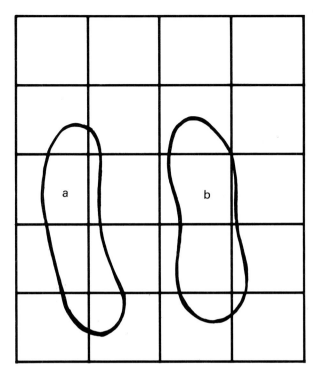

Banana pattern pieces

a Cut three pieces in cream coloured felt.
b Banana skin: cut four pieces in yellow felt.

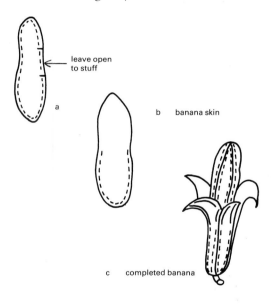

Diagram 47   Construction of banana

115

23

MOTHER
AND
BABY
ELEPHANT

MOTHER
ELEPHANT

SIZE
Length 36.8cm (14½in); height 33.6cm (13¼in)

GRADING
Moderately difficult

TECHNIQUES
Bulk filling and the need to retain a good shape to
the toy; the comparison between a large and a small
elephant made to a similar construction; application
of felt toe-nails

DESIGN BRIEF
Two toys which would provide a contrast between
making and handling a large shape in relation to a
small one

**EVALUATION AND DEVELOPMENT
OF DESIGN**
In their natural environment, the very young
elephants can often be seen holding on to their
mothers' tails by their trunks. These designs of a
toy elephant and baby developed from such a

Figure 33. Elephant and baby

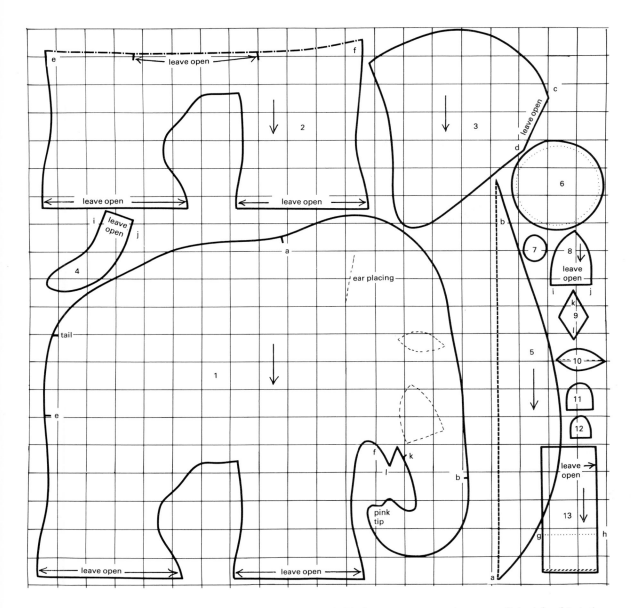

Mother elephant pattern pieces

1 Body: cut two in grey polished fur fabric (one reversed).

2 Underbody gusset: cut two in grey polished fur fabric (one reversed).

3 Ears: cut four in grey polished fur fabric (one reversed).

4 Tusks: cut four in white felt.

5 Head gusset: cut one in grey polished fur fabric.

6 Foot pads: cut four in grey felt. Cut four in cardboard to the size of the dotted inner circle.

7 Trunk tip: cut one in pale pink felt.

8 Tusk cover: cut two in grey polished fur fabric (one reversed).

9 Mouth lining: cut one in pale pink felt.

10 Eye bases: cut three in grey felt. One piece is cut in half where indicated by the broken line – these are the eyelids. Cut one in black felt; cut this in half, fringe for the lashes and insert under the eyelid, then stitch in place.

11 Toe-nails: cut four in white felt.

12 Toe-nails: cut four in white felt.

13 Tail: cut one piece in grey polished fur fabric. Cut a piece of black shaggy pile fur fabric size from g-h to the end gathering line.

117

photograph seen in an animal encyclopaedia. So many toy elephant patterns have already been designed that, at first, whilst the subject seemed suitable to meet the design brief, it was difficult to imagine a toy elephant subject which had not already been made. Once the photograph was seen the project quickly took place.

CHOICE OF MATERIALS
Polished fur fabric is essential for both subjects as this produces the correct appearance of a smooth skin. Long pile acrylic fur fabric produces a perfect tuft at the end of each elephant's tail.

MATERIALS REQUIRED
Grey polished fur fabric 76.2cm (30in) × 71.2cm (28in)

White felt for the tusks and toe-nails 25.4cm (10in) × 14cm (5½in)

Grey felt for the foot base 17.8cm (7in) × 17.8cm (7in)

Two oddments of grey felt measuring 5cm (2in) × 2.5cm (1in) for the eye backs

Pink felt for the tip of the trunk – a 2.5cm (1in) diameter circle

An oddment of pink felt measuring 5cm (2in) × 2.5cm (1in) for the nose piece

A piece of black long pile fur fabric 5cm (2in) × 3.8cm (1½in) for the tail tip

One pair of blue safety lock eyes size 16mm

Toy filling – it is more satisfactory to use a very lightweight filling due to the extreme bulk of this elephant.

CONSTRUCTION
Cut out all the pattern pieces as listed.

Underbody gusset With the right sides facing, pin then backstitch together from (e) to (f), leaving a stuffing opening where indicated on the pattern.

Body With the right sides facing, place the two body pieces together and pin from under the chin to (l) and from (k) to the trunk tip, leaving the trunk tip open. Continue pinning the body together to (b). Insert the head gusset between the body pieces, matching (b-a) on the head gusset to (b-a) on both sides of the body.

Continue to pin the body together to (e). Backstitch where pinned and remove the pins. Insert the underbody gusset, matching the right sides of the gusset to the right sides of the body; (e-f) on the underbody gusset should connect to (e-f)

on the body. Pin into place and then backstitch, leaving the straight edges at each leg base open.

Insert the felt end piece to the curved ends of the trunk; pin then backstitch into place. Insert the mouth piece matching (l-k) on the mouth piece to (l-k) on the body. Pin then backstitch.

Foot pads Place a cardboard lining on to each foot pad and use Copydex to glue a card lining to the centre of each pad, leaving the outside edges free from the adhesive. When dry, insert a pad into each leg base; pin then backstitch.

It is essential, when placing these bases into position in the legs, that the card lining is placed centrally in each leg base and that the leg skin is stitched to the base up to the edge of the card lining, because otherwise the result will be a soft edge all around the foot base.

Turn the body to the right side. Insert the safety lock eyes, placing a felt eye base behind each eye. Stuff the toy carefully and make sure the outside skin surface feels smooth to the touch. It is advisable to lay the toy aside for a day or two to let the toy filling settle, then stuff again firmly. Close the stuffing opening using ladder stitching.

Eyelids and lashes Cut out one eye backing pattern in black felt. Cut in half where indicated on the pattern. Snip into each long straight edge to form the lashes. Ladder stitch the curved edge on each eyelid to the body immediately above the eyes.

Tusks Place together in pairs. Overstitch around the outside edges, leaving open the top straight edge on each. Stuff firmly up to the dotted line (i-j) and stitch across this line. Ladder stitch this unfilled top section to the head where indicated on the pattern.

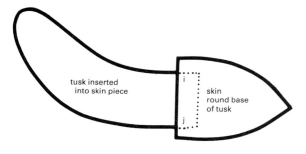

Diagram 48   Elephant tusk placing

Ladder stitch a fur fabric skin covering round the base of each tusk over the flat tusk top section, matching (i-j) on skin to (i-j) on each tusk. Before finally closing each skin, insert a small amount of toy filling to add shaping.

Ears With right sides facing, place the ear pieces together in pairs. Pin then backstitch around the outside edge leaving (c-d) open. Turn to the right side. Overstitch (c-d) to close, and ladder stitch the ears on either side of the body where indicated on the pattern.

Tail Add a black piece of long pile acrylic fur fabric to the tail at (g-h), making sure that the pile line on the two tail pieces match. Fold the tail in half lengthways with the wrong sides facing. Stitch the seams together and then fold the tail lengthways a second time, encasing the previously stitched seam. Ladder stitch together the folded length of the tail. The tail skin forms its own filling. Ladder stitch to the body.

Toe-nails These are ladder stitched into place on the toy skin (see Diagram 49). Stitch one side of the felt nail, then allow the felt to bulge into a tube shape which is then ladder stitched all around the outside curve, leaving the bottom edge open. Stuff the tube with toy filling. Cut a half circle of felt to fit the nail base formed by the tube. Overstitch into place. Treat all the toe-nails in the same way.

Finally, examine the elephant to see whether the legs splay out from the body. Some underbodies are darted to prevent this happening. At the design stage of this elephant, it was found that all that was required to make it stand firmly was a small curve

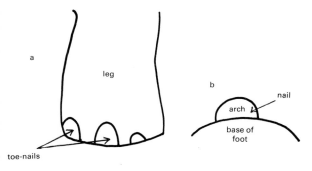

Diagram 49 Elephant's toe-nails (not to scale). a) white felt toe-nail placing. b) View from base of the foot, showing arch formed by the felt toe-nail and nail base.

of ladder stitching making a small dart behind each leg, applied after the toy was made up.

It is essential to groom both the elephants carefully to produce smoothness of the toy skin.

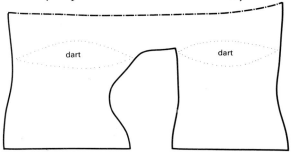

Diagram 50 Darting an underbody gusset to prevent the legs splaying out

BABY ELEPHANT

SIZE
Length 25.4cm (10in), height 17.8cm (7in)

MATERIALS REQUIRED
Grey polished fur fabric measuring 55.9cm (22in) × 33cm (13in)
Grey felt for the footpads, four 3.3cm (1¼in) diameter circles
Oddment of black shaggy long pile fur fabric for the tail tuft
One pair of blue safety lock eyes size 10mm
Toy filling
A pipe-cleaner
Pieces of strong card for the foot base lining

CONSTRUCTION
Cut out all the pattern pieces as listed.

Underbody With the right sides facing, pin then backstitch the underbody gusset together at (c-d), leaving a stuffing opening where indicated on the pattern.

Body Place the body pieces together with the right sides facing and pin from under the chin to (e1) then from (e) to (h) and (g) to (a). Insert the head gusset matching (a-b) on both sides. Continue to pin the body pieces together from (b) to (f). Backstitch where pinned.

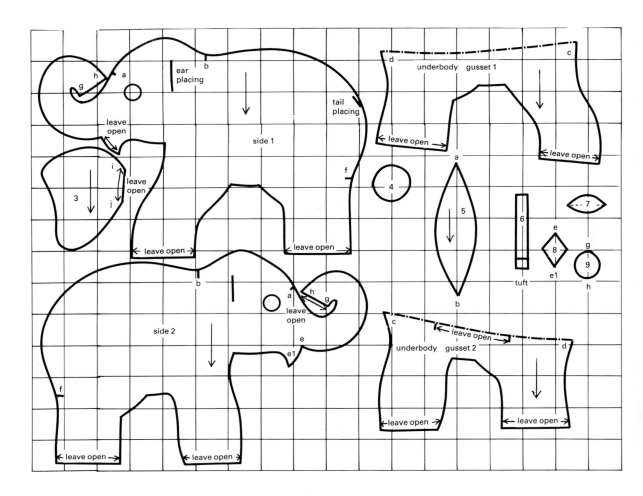

Baby elephant pattern pieces

1 Body side: cut one in light grey polished fur fabric.
2 Body side: cut one in light grey polished fur fabric.
1 Underbody gusset: cut one in light grey polished fur fabric.
2 Underbody gusset: cut one in light grey polished fur fabric.
3 Ears: cut four in light grey polished fur fabric (two reversed).

4 Foot pads: cut four in grey or pink felt.
5 Head gusset: cut one in light grey polished fur fabric.
6 Tail: cut one in light grey felt. Cut the tuft in black shaggy fur fabric.
7 Eye backs: cut two in light grey felt for the eye backs, and cut one pattern in black felt to be cut in half for the eyelashes.
8 Mouth: cut one in pale pink felt.
9 Trunk end: cut one in pale pink felt.

Remove the pins and insert the underbody gusset between the two body pieces, with the right sides of the gusset facing the right sides of the body skin, matching body side 1 to underbody gusset 1 and body side 2 to underbody side 2. Pin into place then backstitch, leaving the straight edges at each leg base open.

Pin the felt mouth piece into place, matching (e) to (e) and (e1) to (e1). Insert the felt trunk end piece at (gh). Backstitch both the mouth piece and the trunk end piece and remove the pins. Pin and then backstitch the felt foot bases into place. Turn the body to the right side.

Insert the safety lock eyes placing a felt eye base behind each eye. Place a card lining inside each felt foot pad. Stuff the elephant firmly and close the stuffing opening using ladder stitching.

Eyelids and lashes Cut out one eye backing pattern in black felt. Cut in half where indicated on the pattern. Snip into each long straight edge to form the lashes. Ladder stitch the curved edge on each eyelid to the body immediately above each eye.

Ears With the right sides facing, place together in pairs. Pin then backstitch leaving (i–j) open. Turn to the right side. Close the opening (i–j) on each ear and ladder stitch in place on the body where indicated on the pattern.

Tail Stitch a small tuft of long pile acrylic fur fabric to one short end on the felt tail piece. Lay a pipe-cleaner, cut to the size of the felt tail piece, on to the wrong side of the felt tail; fold the felt around the pipe-cleaner and overstitch to secure. Ladder stitch the tail to the body where indicated.

24
LION
CUB

SIZE
Length of body 48.2cm (19in)

GRADING
Moderately difficult

TECHNIQUES
Basic needlemodelling
Stuffing a lying–down toy which has a shaped gusset comprising several pieces. Pad marking application

DESIGN BRIEF
A lying–down toy to demonstrate body and gusset shaping – to be washable, soft, cuddly and suitable for most age groups

EVALUATION OF DESIGN BRIEF
Soft equals texture, whatever age we are we instinctively feel or touch an article. Take care, however, when stuffing a toy that 'soft' does not

Figure 34. Lion cub

122

mean under-stuffed. Softness also relates to cuddly.

Washable is almost self-explanatory – all the materials should be washable and should return to their original appearance: the washing should not be detrimental to the toy.

CHOICE OF MATERIALS

Short pile fur fabric in a light fawn colour is most suitable. Terylene toy filling is lightweight and washable. Whereas felt has usually been omitted from washable toys, due to the fact that it is composed of fibres impacted together and therefore does not wash well, advances have been made and some felts are blended on to a backing and can be washed.

MATERIALS REQUIRED

Body Fawn coloured short pile fur fabric 96.5cm (38in) × 63.5cm (25in)

Pads Light beige felt 10.3cm (4in) × 22.3cm (8¾in)

Nose, eyelashes and pad markings Dark beige felt 7.6cm (3in) × 7.6cm (3in)

Eye base White felt 5cm (2in) × 5cm (2in)

Eye Yellow felt 5cm (2in) × 5cm (2in)

Eyelids Oddments of fawn coloured felt to match the body fabric

Eye pupil Oddments of black felt

Chin piece Polished white fur fabric 3.8cm (1½in) × 9.6cm (3¾in)

Whiskers Horsehair

Toy filling: terylene

CONSTRUCTION

Cut out all the pattern pieces as listed.

Head gusset Construct the gusset by matching (b) to (b) and (c-c) to (c-c). Stitch to join. With the right sides of the side head pieces facing, insert the head gusset between the side head pieces from the base of the neck (a) round to the back of the neck (d); pin then backstitch in place. Turn to the right side. Stuff firmly. Gather around the neck edge, pull up

slightly and add more filling but do not close completely. Fasten off.

Ears With the right sides facing, place together in pairs; pin then backstitch around the outside edges to join leaving the bottom straight edges open. Turn to the right side. Overstitch the open edges to join and pull up slightly to curve. Fasten off. Pin in place on the stuffed head.

Eyes Construct as shown on pattern. Pin in place on the head.

Nose shaping The bridge of the nose is shaped by taking stitches from one side to the other and pulling them up to form a ridge. The distance across is approximately 3.8cm (1½in) and starts about 4.5cm (1¾in) from the top of the white fur fabric on the gusset, and is worked to a length of approximately 7.6cm (3in).

When satisfied that the ears and eyes are correctly placed, using Figure 34 to aid placing, ladder stitch the ears in place, then ladder stitch the eyes, adding a small amount of filling behind each eye piece prior to closing. Using a neat running stitch, attach the eyelashes to the eyelids, then stitch the top of each eyelid in place above each eye, following the top curve of the eye shape.

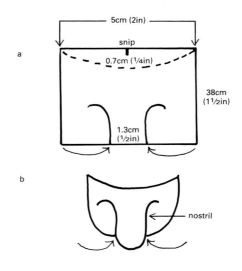

Diagram 51 Lion cub's nose. a) Measurements for nose piece – curved arrows indicate folding to form the front of the nose. b) Showing formed nose and nostrils.

Nose Cut a 5cm (2in) × 3.8cm (1½in) piece of dark beige felt. Snip at the top centre where indicated on Diagram 51, and fold in the top edge into a curve 0.7cm (¼in) in the centre graduating at each corner. Take the bottom corners and tuck them behind the 1.3cm (½in) centre piece; pin into place, thus forming a fold on either side which are the nostrils. Ladder stitch the nose in place, stuffing before finally closing; the centre of the bottom edge of the felt nose is approximately 2.5cm (1in) from the top of the white fur fabric chin piece.

Body With the right sides facing, pin and stitch (e–f) to (e–f) on the back inner leg pieces (see Diagram 52). Insert and pin these between the back legs of the body pieces with the right sides facing. Pin then backstitch around the outside of the body to join together, leaving open where indicated on the back legs (g–h) and on the body stuffing opening. Insert a foot pad into each back leg, pin then backstitch.

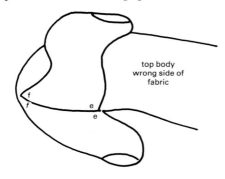

Diagram 52 Placing of inner leg pieces

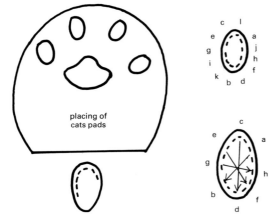

Diagram 53 Placing of cat's pads: lettering indicates the order of stitching around a pad for ease of application

Turn the body to the right side, stuff the body and top leg firmly but leave the underfoot lightly, but evenly, stuffed to enable the top leg to lie flat. Be careful when stuffing a lying-down toy which has one back leg under the other not to overstuff the underleg in depth, as this will result in the top leg lying too high. Close the stuffing opening with ladder stitching.

Ladder stitch the front pads into place where indicated on the pattern. Using dark beige felt and small running stitches add the pad markings. Ladder stitch the prepared head into place where indicated; it may be necessary to work a second line of ladder stitching around the neck to produce a firm head attachment.

Tail With the right sides facing, fold in half lengthways and backstitch the edges together, closing one end with gathering. Turn to the right side. Making sure the pile line on the tail follows on the pile line on the body, ladder stitch to the body where indicated.

Whiskers Apply on either side of the nose.

Lion cub pattern pieces

1 Underbody: cut one in light beige fur fabric.
2 Inside leg for underbody: cut one in light beige fur fabric.
3 Side head: cut two in light beige fur fabric (one reversed).
4 Back leg foot pads: cut two in medium beige felt.
5 Eye combination: a) pupils: cut two in black felt; b) complete piece: cut two in yellow felt; c) complete piece: cut two in white felt.
6 Eyelashes: cut two in dark beige felt. Cut where indicated.
7 Eyelids: cut two in light beige felt.
8 Front leg foot pads: cut two in medium beige felt.
9 Chin piece: cut one in white polished fur fabric.
10 Back of head gusset: cut one in light beige fur fabric.
11 Ears: cut four in light beige fur fabric (two reversed).
12 Top body: cut one in light beige fur fabric. Measure 10.3cm (4in) from the inside curve of the front legs straight on to the body, and mark; this will indicate the approximate placing of the front neck edge of the head when placed on the body at the completion stage.
13 Top body inside leg: cut one in light beige fur fabric.
14 Head gusset: cut one in light beige fur fabric. Join the cut out head gusset fur fabric pattern pieces 14, 10 and 9 to make the complete gusset.
15 Paw markings: cut a set for each foot pad.

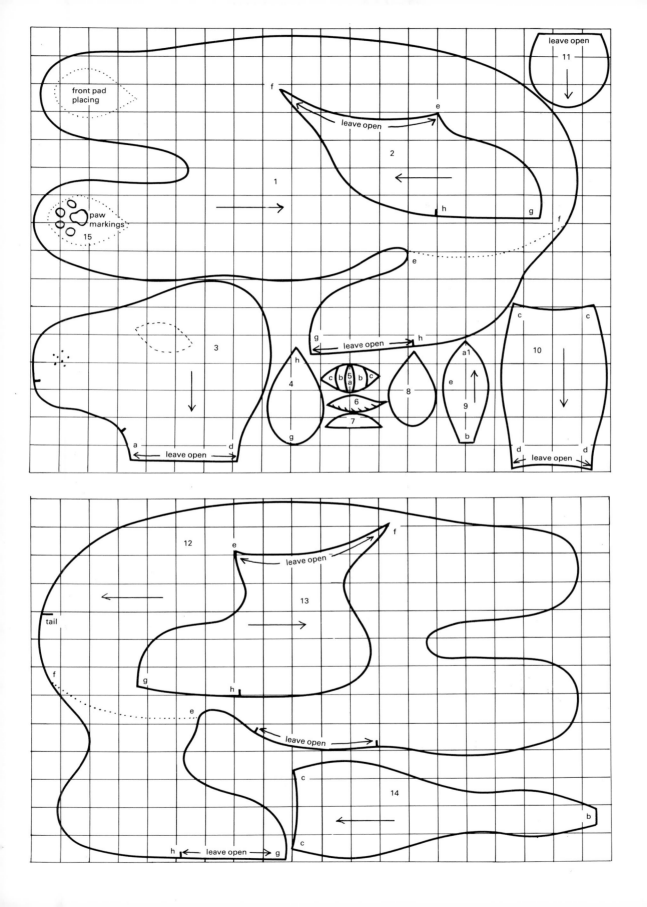

25
LONG
NECK
BLACK
CAT

SIZE
Height 35.5cm (14in)

GRADING
Easy

TECHNIQUES
Felt composition eye. Balance. Careful shaping

DESIGN BRIEF
A toy using a china ornament as inspiration

EVALUATION OF DESIGN BRIEF
When design inspiration seems elusive, it can be quite a good exercise to look around the home. Sometimes all that is required is a brief glance at an object and an idea will start to form. Just as an art teacher might supply a model or article for the students to draw, an ornament or model can be supplied to a class of toymakers for them to design a toy. The long neck cat developed using a china ornament as the inspiration and adapting the shape until it became possible to turn the design into a toy.

DEVELOPMENT OF DESIGN
Care had to be taken to produce a well-balanced toy. When a design has a long neck on a comparatively small base, it is very easy for the toy to topple over. This can sometimes be rectified by adding a weight at the base, well covered and secure, taking into consideration safety factors. Another method can be to use a heavier type of toy filling for the base and lighter weight for the neck and head.

CHOICE OF MATERIALS
Polished fur fabric was used to produce the correct sleek feel to the cat's coat; the smoothness of the fabric helped to produce a good outline shape to the toy. This also connected up well with the china ornament model. When developing a design, care must be taken to choose the correct materials, because otherwise the transposition from a china shape into a soft toy model shape could lose all the visual impact of the original model.

When making a toy in dark coloured fabric, the eyes can easily become lost. With a cat subject, yellow or green eye colouring can be used, both of which show up well.

Figure 35.   Long neck black cat

MATERIALS REQUIRED

Fur fabric A piece of polished fur fabric 48.2cm (19in) × 48.2cm (19in)

Felt Oddments of black felt for ears
Pink felt for ear lining, nose and tongue
Green and yellow felt for eyes

Braid Oddment of braid approximately 2.5cm (1in) × 10.9cm (4¼in) for collar

Sewing thread
Toy filling
Horsehair for whiskers
Piece of strong card slightly smaller than the base pattern

CONSTRUCTION
Cut out all the pattern pieces as listed.

Body With right sides facing, pin then stitch the curved back seams together from top of neck to tail base. Insert the front body gusset (for placing see graph layout). Backstitch these seams, leaving the top of the neck and the base open.

Insert the base, the straight edge to the front of the body, and the curve to the base at the back. Stitch round this base leaving one side open. Turn to the right side and insert the cardboard base cut slightly smaller all round than the fur fabric base. Ladder stitch the opening together to close.

Stuff the cat firmly, paying careful attention to shaping. When moulded and shaped satisfactorily, close the narrow top neck opening using a running stitch to gather round the top edge. Before finally closing, add more stuffing, as this part of the toy must be very firm in order to take the head.

Head Using small running stitches, gather round the outside edge of the 17.8cm (7in) diameter fur fabric circle. Pull up slightly and stuff firmly, making sure you have achieved a good head shape. Pull the gathers to fit the top of the neck. Fasten then ladder stitch the head to the neck. If necessary, go round with your stitching a second time.

Ears For each ear, place one black and one pink ear piece together. Stitch the curved sides together using stab stitching; fasten the thread but do not detach. Overstitch the bottom straight edge of the ear and pull up slightly to form a gentle curve. Fasten off. Pin to the head.

Eyes Construct the eyes as in Diagram 54. Pin to the head using Figure 35 as a guide to placing. The reason for pinning the ears and eyes in position is so that you can move them until you are satisfied that they are well placed; then remove the pins and stitch into place. Add eyelashes along the top of each eye, using a small running stitch, and starting at the inside point on each eye and working outwards.

Add the nose and tongue using small neat stitches.

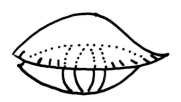

Diagram 54   Eye construction

Whiskers Apply the whiskers using light-coloured horsehair on dark fur fabric, or vice versa, to show up well.

Tail Fold in half lengthways and backstitch the seams together, leaving the top straight edge open. Turn to the right side and stuff firmly, forming it into a curve as you stuff so that the tail fits the base of the body shape. Close the opening by gathering using small running stitches and ladder stitch to the centre at the base of the back. Curve the tail around the body base and stitch into place.

Finally, add the braid collar and stitch to hold in place at the back of the neck by neatly folding in any raw edges. It can accentuate the eye colouring if the braid chosen is in green and gold for a cat with green and yellow eyes, and similarly a braid to match whatever eye colouring chosen.

Brush the body and tail smoothly following the fur fabric pile line to produce a sleek appearance. Brush the head following the pile line, but brushing out the fur pile into a cat like shape at the cheeks.

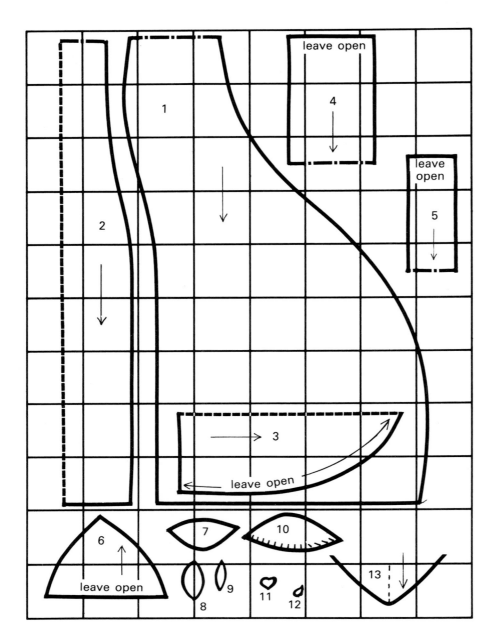

Cat pattern pieces

1 Body: add pattern piece No. 4 to No. 1 to make complete pattern, then cut two in fur fabric (one reversed).

2 Front body gusset: add pattern piece No. 5 to No. 2 to make complete pattern, then cut one in fur fabric.

3 Base: cut one in fur fabric.

4 and 5 See above.

6 Ears: cut two in black felt and two in pink felt for the ear linings.

7 Ear bases: cut two in bright green felt.

8 Eye centres: cut two in yellow felt.

9 Eye pupils: cut two in black felt.

10 Eyelid and lashes combination: cut two in black felt.

11 Nose: cut one in pink felt.

12 Tongue: cut one in pink felt.

13 Tail: cut one in fur fabric 5cm (2in) × 22.9cm (9in); curve to form tail tip (see pattern).

14 Head: cut one 17.8cm (7in) diameter circle in fur fabric.

26
SEAL
AND
BABY

SIZE
Height 33cm (13in), body length 34.3cm (13½in)

GRADING
Easy

TECHNIQUES
Applying whiskers. Wiring flippers. Shading using fabric paint. Design illustrating the necessity of good internal shaping with toy filling

DESIGN BRIEF
A basic toy with a clear body line to enable the maximum of shaping to be achieved by the toy filling

EVALUATION OF DESIGN BRIEF
The seal as a subject has a very basic outline shape; the end product relies on good stuffing techniques to produce an appealing and impressive toy.

Figure 36.   Seal and baby

CHOICE OF MATERIALS

Polished fur fabric has a smooth shiny surface which simulates the skin of the seal. Nylon or terylene toy filling is suitable if the toy is to be washable. Kapok could be used if the toy is to be a model rather than a plaything.

MATERIALS REQUIRED

Polished light grey fur fabric 45.7cm (18in) × 76.2cm (30in)

Flippers, tail and ear linings Dark grey felt 60.9cm (24in) × 15.3cm (6in)
One safety lock nose size 20mm
One pair of safety lock eyes, blue size 14mm
Horsehair for the whiskers
Sixteen pipe-cleaners for stiffening the flippers and tail
Toy filling

SEAL

CONSTRUCTION

Cut out all the pattern pieces as listed.

Body With the right sides of the fur fabric facing, pin then backstitch together from (a) at the throat, over the head and down the back to the tail (b). Insert the underbody gusset by pinning then backstitching between (a) and (b), leaving one body seam open where indicated at the base near the tail as a stuffing opening. Turn to the right side.

Insert the safety lock eyes and the nose. Stuff the body firmly, taking care to produce a smooth surface to the toy skin; using ladder stitching, close the stuffing opening.

Ears Place one fur fabric and one felt lining together, right sides facing, leaving (c–d) open for turning. Pin then backstitch together. Turn to the right side and ladder stitch to the head where indicated on the pattern, with the fur fabric side of the ear lining up to the body pile (see Diagram 55). Treat the other ear in the same way.

Flippers Place the pattern pieces together in pairs. Pin together around the outside edges, leaving the top straight (e–f) open. Stab stitch around the outside edge of each pair. Insert three pipe-cleaners into each flipper, as indicated on Diagram 56; trim to the required length, if necessary. Stab stitch down both sides of each pipe-cleaner to hold in place.

Figure 37. Seal

Lay the top section of a flipper on one side of the body where indicated and ladder stitch (e1) to (e), (e) to (f), and (f) to (f1). Stitch across (f1) to (e1) using a running stitch. Treat the other flipper on the opposite side of the body in the same way.

Place a flipper top cover with the pile on the right side, over the stitched top of a flipper, matching the lines (e1) to (f1). Ladder stitch in place. Prior to closing the line (e1) to (f1), apply a small amount of toy filling to add shaping. Treat the opposite flipper in the same way.

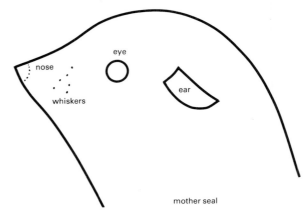

Diagram 55 Feature placing for mother seal

130

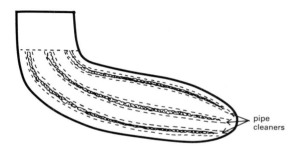

Diagram 56 Stiffening placing in a flipper

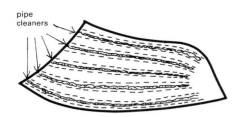

Diagram 57 Stiffening placing in a tail

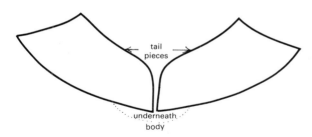

Diagram 58 View from underbody of the tail placing

Tail Place the felt pattern pieces together in pairs and stab stitch each pair together around the outside edges, leaving (g) to (h) open. Insert five pipe-cleaners cut to length into each tail piece, and stab stitch down both sides of each pipe-cleaner to hold in place.

Close (g) to (h) with ladder stitching, and attach a tail piece on either side of the body where indicated; top ladder stitch each tail piece to secure to the body.

Whiskers Apply the whiskers where indicated on Diagram 55 (if referring to the previous book, use Method 1, p. 83).

BABY SEAL

Figure 38. Baby seal made in white fur fabric

SIZE
28cm (11in) long

GRADING
Easy

MATERIALS REQUIRED
Polished fur fabric 66cm (26in) × 38.1cm (15in)
One pair of safety lock eyes, blue, size 12mm
One safety lock nose size 15mm
Toy filling
Horsehair for whiskers

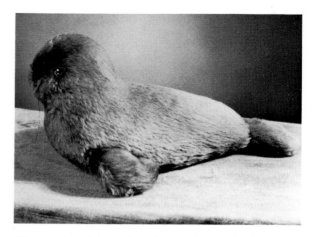

Figure 39. Baby seal made in dark grey fur fabric

131

CONSTRUCTION

Cut out the pattern pieces as listed.

Body With the right sides facing, pin the body pieces together from (a–b) over the top of the body. Insert the underbody gusset matching (a–b) on the gusset to (a–b) on the body, leaving a stuffing opening where indicated on the pattern. Backstitch seams and remove the pins. Turn to the right side and insert the safety lock eyes where indicated on the pattern. Insert the safety lock nose at point (a).

Stuff the body firmly, paying careful attention to the skin surface which should be completely smooth to the touch. Close the stuffing opening with ladder stitching.

Tail Place the tail pieces together in pairs with right sides facing. Pin then backstitch around the outside of each, leaving the top straight edge open to allow for turning. Turn to the right side. Do not stuff.

Overstitch the straight edges to close the stuffing opening. Ladder stitch the tail pieces at (b) on to the body, making sure that the outer curve on each tail piece is to the outside.

Flipper With right sides facing, place the flipper pieces together in pairs. Pin then stitch around the outside edge leaving the top straight edge open for turning. Turn to the right side and stuff. Close the opening with ladder stitching, and ladder stitch to the body using Figure 39 to aid placing.

Whiskers Using horsehair and Method 1, apply the whiskers where indicated on the pattern.

Baby seal pattern pieces

1 Body: cut two in polished fur fabric (one reversed).
2 Underbody gusset: cut one in polished fur fabric.
3 Tail: cut four in polished fur fabric (two reversed).
4 Flippers: cut four in polished fur fabric (two reversed).

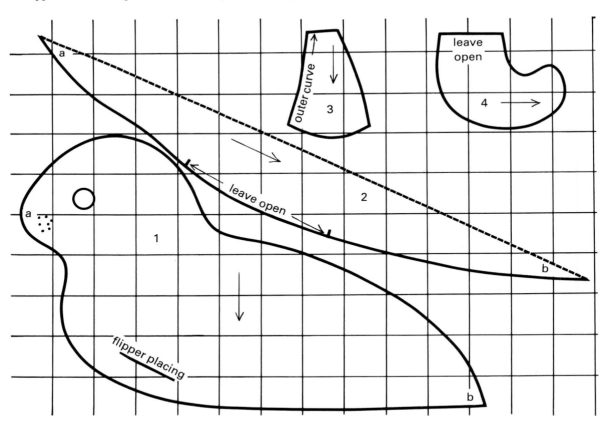

132

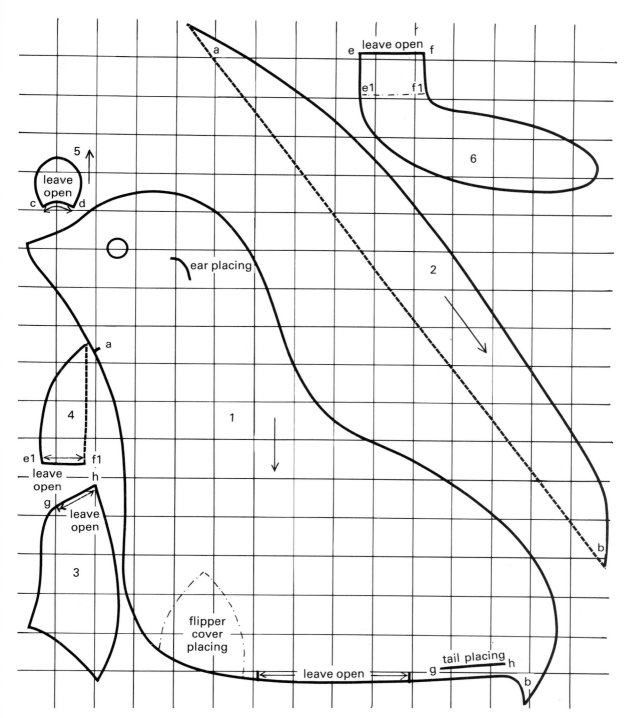

Mother seal pattern pieces

1 Body: cut two in polished grey fur fabric (one reversed).

2 Underbody gusset: cut one in polished grey fur fabric.

3 Tail: cut four in grey felt.

4 Top cover for flippers: cut two in polished grey fur fabric.

5 Ears: cut two in polished grey fur fabric and two ear linings in grey felt.

6 Flippers: cut four in grey felt.

133

APPENDIX I

EQUIPMENT AND MATERIALS REQUIRED FOR SOFT TOYMAKING

Sewing box items

Sewing needles including a curved needle
Scissors
Pinking shears
Pins, preferably with coloured heads
Tape measure
Tailor's chalk in light and dark colours
Variety of sewing threads
Soft pencils
Assorted embroidery threads

Pattern-making materials

All-purpose glue, for example UHU, Bostik No.1,
    Elmers Glue-All
Graph paper
Tracing or greaseproof paper
Hard pencils
Pair of compasses
Card for mounting patterns
Scissors: keep these for paper cutting and avoid using
    material cutting scissors
Set square with right angle
Adhesive tape
Paper clips
Pencil sharpener

Stuffing a toy

Variety of different size stuffing sticks: these can be
made of dowelling, wooden knitting needles, wooden
meat skewers, toothpicks, forceps or wooden sticks
with a notch cut in the top
Teazle brush for final grooming
Variety of toy fillings: avoid foam chips as these are
messy to use; Kapok is useful for filling small awkward
places and as a base on a toy face to provide a good
surface for embroidering features, but it is very fly-away
and gets into one's eyes and nose. Terylene or nylon
fillings are easier to use and these are washable.

Jointing a toy

A selection of disc joints
Thin round-nosed pliers
Polyfil 25 thread or button thread for stitched hinging

Wiring

Pipe-cleaners
Galvanized wire no.16 gauge
Adhesive tape, either medical or electrical
Thin round-nosed pliers
Wire cutters

Felt feature application

If gluing, not stitching, features, use Copydex glue.
This latex-based adhesive becomes absorbed into the
felt and the adhesion to the face mask is very strong.
Many glues are only absorbed into the top surface of the
felt, which then enables it to be easily removed by tiny
fingers.

Laminating a mask

Polycell paste
Plasticine

Safety lock eyes and noses

A selection of safety lock eyes and noses, and the tool to
apply those designs which are too strong to apply by
hand
Wire cutters
Screw driver to prise off eye backs when the eyes have
been placed in the wrong position
Iron-on Vylene to support loosely woven fabric backs
to enable firm eye application

It is not necessary to purchase all the above items at
one time. As with any craft, start with the basic requirements for the toys you have chosen to make, and the
equipment will gradually build up over a period of time.
Also be versatile and, where possible, substitute items
when required. For example, greaseproof paper can be
used for tracing patterns rather than tracing paper.

I find it useful to collect circular household jar and tin lids; mark them on the top with their diameter size, and these can be used in place of a pair of compasses. Card for mounting patterns may be available in your home as cereal boxes. Pliers may already be part of a household tool-box.

Organisation and storage of materials

Whatever the craft you are pursuing, and toymaking is no exception, do try and be organised: tidiness is the essence of organisation. To work in a constant muddle can produce items to a poor standard and be a great timewaster – always turning work over to look for a particular piece of equipment; there is also the added danger of pins and needles being caught up in the toy.

Toy patterns
Starting with the toy patterns: keep each pattern separately, either in a folder or envelope, or secured with a pipe-cleaner by making a hole in each pattern piece and threading it on to the pipe-cleaner and twisting the end to secure. Whatever method used, label each pattern clearly. Some of my students keep their patterns in clear A-4 size plastic pocket envelopes and place these in ring binders; as their collection increases they add further folders.

Sewing items
Organisation of sewing items is very much a personal choice, from a work basket to a plastic tool-box.

Various equipment
Pliers, hammer, and the heavier equipment can be stored and carried around in plastic tool-boxes which are very inexpensive and available from D.I.Y. stores.

Maintenance
From time to time, check over and tidy any equipment. It can be very frustrating to settle down to make a toy only to find that none of your pencils has a good point and your pencil sharpener not to hand.

Storing of materials

This can present a problem. Most of us are restricted in our homes to the space we can allocate for our craft materials, especially if more than one craft subject is pursued at a time. A craft can quickly lead to the extension to other subjects with subsequent build-up of equipment and materials.

Fur fabrics and toy fillings are both bulky. These can be stored in large plastic bags in a garage or garden shed. A word of caution: do not place the bags too near a window as sun on plastic bags will produce moisture inside, with obvious results. When storing fur fabric, try and roll rather than fold each piece as this avoids permanent creasing to the pile. Store all dark and all light fabrics separately to avoid fluff from one pile colour getting on to another.

Costwise, to purchase larger quantities of toymaking materials is beneficial, and, with care taken over storing the items, they can be stored for some long time without losing their freshness.

Safety lock eyes and noses can be stored in tins according to their mm size, colour and type, which should be clearly stated on the outside.

Disc joint sets should be stored in plastic bags; this will avoid the cotter pins becoming rusty, which they quickly do if exposed to the damp.

APPENDIX II

GENERAL TOYMAKING TECHNIQUES

Instructions on patterns

Many mistakes can be avoided if all instructions (for example, pile line arrows, name of toy, part of toy, number of pieces, material to be used) are marked on to the pattern when tracing or designing them. It is a good policy to mark on the reverse side of the pattern those pieces which require to be reversed, or to have a second copy of the pattern piece cut out and marked in the reverse position.

Enlarging and reducing a pattern

There are three methods for achieving this, but the basic theory is that you change the scale of the grid from which the pattern is to be copied and either enlarge or reduce it in size. Work square to square, copying your pattern outline on to the new grid size.

Graph paper, marked with grids of varying sizes, is available from stationers or stores which stock dressmaking requirements; but to save money and time it is useful to make a master copy which can then be fixed on to a board and covered with clear plastic adhesive sheeting, the type used for covering book covers. All that is then required is tracing paper to lay over the grid and to copy your pattern.

Once mounted on card, the pattern can be used as a template to cut out large quantities of patterns, if required, or can be passed from one person to another without fear of the pattern deteriorating. One point to add: when tracing a pattern from one which has been mounted on cardboard, the new outline tends to become larger. One often finds, after a number of subsequent tracings have been made, that not only has the toy become appreciably larger, but also – in extreme cases – that the original amount of material quoted is no longer sufficient for the toy!

Method 1

Many books and magazines have their toy patterns produced on a small scale, set on squares. It is then

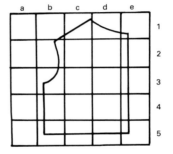

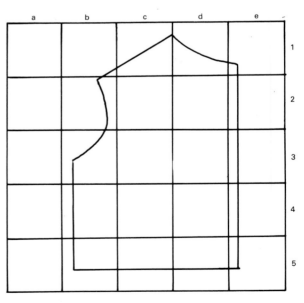

Diagram 59 Enlarging and reducing a pattern: Method 1

necessary to enlarge the pattern pieces to their correct size by enlarging on to graph paper. Usually the small pattern states, for example, 'each square represents 2.5cm (1in)', and therefore it is necessary either to purchase some 2.5cm (1in) graph paper to enlarge on to or to draw 2.5cm (1in) squares on plain paper.

Accuracy in drawing your squares is essential. The size of the paper is determined by the number of squares on the small graph layout. When enlarging the design a great deal it helps to number the squares down one side and letter the squares across the top. Also number and letter the corresponding squares on the small layout. Re-draw the pattern pieces on to the enlarged sheet, using your lettering and numbering to assist in re-drawing accurately: care at this stage will result in an exact copy.

Some people find it assists them if they add dots where the lines of the pattern cross the lines on the squared paper and then carefully draw and connect between the dots. To reduce a large pattern to a smaller size, simply reverse the above process.

If the toy design is not already marked on to a graph, trace the design to be enlarged or reduced, then mark over the design in squares 0.7cm (¼in) or 1.3cm (½in) for small designs and 2.5cm (1in) for large, depending on the size of the design. Then on paper mark large squares – for example to enlarge a design to twice the original size make the squares twice as large. Copy the design as already described

Method 2
For very detailed toy patterns the layout with the extra diagonal lines assists in copying exact details.

Trace the design. Draw a frame around it then draw a

larger frame to the same proportions to fit the desired enlarged size. Draw diagonals corner to corner in each frame; where the diagonals meet is the centre point. To divide equally, draw horizontal and vertical lines. Copy the design from the small version to the large one.

Method 3
Lay a ruler diagonally along (ab); extend beyond (b). Extend line (ac). If you require the enlarged size to measure 30.5cm (12in), continue to extend lines (ab) and (ac) until a line drawn between (d) and (e) measures 30.5cm (12in). This is easily measured by holding a ruler vertically and sliding it across from the line (bc) until it registers 30.5cm (12in) between the line (de).

Complete the outside lines of the enlarged square, rectangle, or whatever shape is being enlarged. Divide this larger square into the same number of small squares as the original one and then proceed to draw the pattern outline, carefully copying the exact portion contained in each of the original small squares.

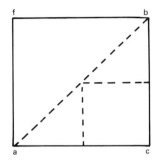

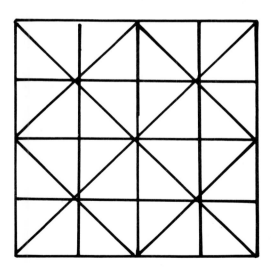

Diagram 60 Enlarging and reducing a pattern: Method 2

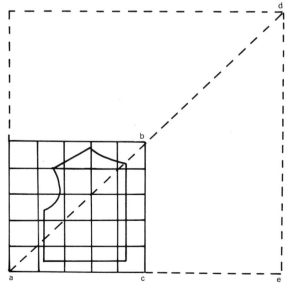

Diagram 61 Enlarging and reducing a pattern: Method 3

137

To reduce a pattern, measure up the side (bc) of the original square to the height to which the reduced toy is to be made; from this point draw a line parallel to top line (f b) of the square as far as the diagonal. From here draw a line parallel to (bc) down to (ac) to complete the new square, which is then divided into the same number of squares as the original one.

Marking out the pattern

Always draw closely to the pattern templates holding the pencil or tailor's chalk in a vertical postion. Make sure there is adequate space to lay out the material. Clearly mark all the annotations on each piece. Never try to mark out a pattern on to creased material.

Draw out the pattern on to the wrong side of the fabric. Dress type materials in cotton or similar can be cut out doubled, but never cut through doubled layers of any fabrics with a nap. Pay careful attention to the design of a patterned fabric in relation to the toy being made; a design can be used to great advantage if limbs, for example, are carefully matched.

Cutting out

Always keep your scissors sharpened. By resting the lower blade on a firm surface or on a finger as support, this will help to control them whilst cutting out. Cut smoothly and avoid making any notches in the cut edge. When using materials which are to be made up on the right side, for example leather or felts, make sure that you remove the drawn outline as you cut the pieces out.

Pinning and tacking (basting)

To ensure well–fitting pattern pieces, pin or tack the pieces together prior to stitching. To obtain a well-balanced gusset, pin one side then back to where you started pinning the gusset, and pin the other side. In the case of a head gusset, for example, pin from the nose to the back of the head, then pin the other side likewise. When stitching, the same principles apply: stitch from the nose to the back of the head, and fasten off. Go back to the nose and stitch the opposite side, from the nose to the back of the head.

Stitching

Loose or uneven stitching will not hold the toy filling. All seaming must be strong enough to withstand the pressure of stuffing the toy. Backstitching produces a good firm outline.

Stuffing

However well a toy is cut out and stitched, poor stuffing methods can spoil the finished article. Stuffing a toy is moulding it from within the toy skin. Firstly the toy filling must be teased out to remove any lumps, then,

using your left hand to hold the part being stuffed (reverse for a left–handed person), insert small pieces of filling with your right hand. A wooden knitting needle or a piece of dowelling is useful to push the filling into any awkward spaces. Scale your needles or dowelling according to the size of toy being stuffed.

If the toy has, for example, a pointed nose, fill this first with small pieces of filling and increase the quantities inserted as the shape broadens out into the bulk of the body. The filling must feel very firm as this will soften as the air is dispelled, and what might at first feel a soft cuddly toy could well end up an almost empty toy skin if under-stuffed in the first place. When making a large toy it is advisable to leave it overnight or longer to allow the filling to settle, before inserting more filling.

The toy is finally ladder stitched to close the stuffing opening. Avoid overstitching an opening to close it, the exception being a toy which has been previously overstitched around the outside edge. For felt toys which have stabbed stitched seams, continue stab stitching to close the stuffing opening, making sure the stab stitching matches the rest of the seaming. A curved needle is useful for those areas which are difficult to work.

Fur fabric

Determine the pile line, i.e. the direction of the pile. Stroke the fabric and, when the pile lays smoothly, that is the pile line. Mark on the back of the fabric with an arrow near the selvedge edge. Another easy method of

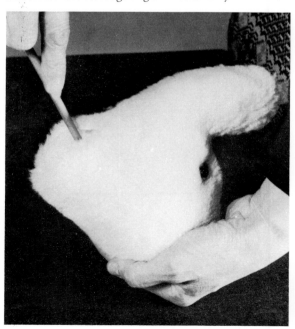

Figure 40. Stuffing an elephant head

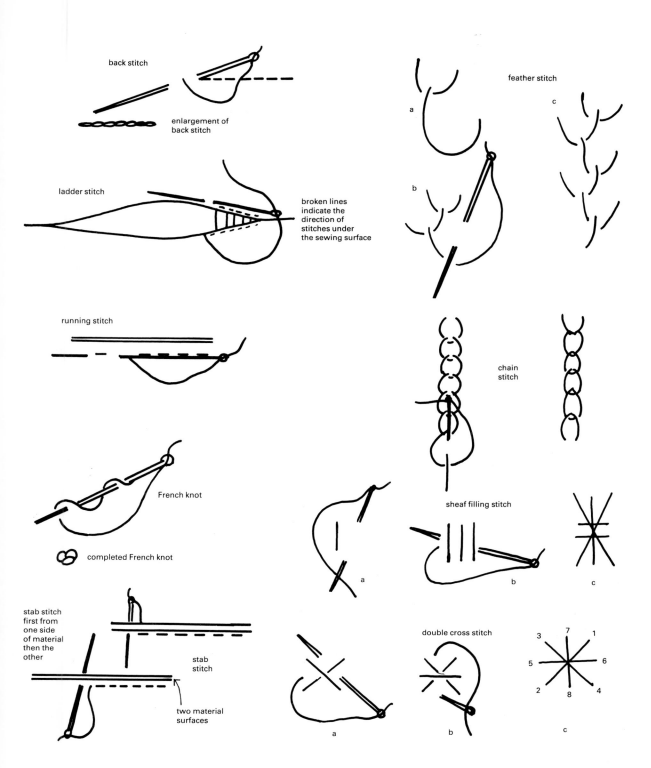

back stitch

enlargement of
back stitch

feather stitch

a

b

c

ladder stitch

broken lines
indicate the
direction of
stitches under
the sewing surface

running stitch

chain
stitch

French knot

sheaf filling stitch

completed French knot

a

b

c

stab stitch
first from
one side
of material
then the
other

stab
stitch

double cross stitch

3   7   1

5   6

2   8   4

two material
surfaces

a

b

c

Diagram 62   A variety of stitches

139

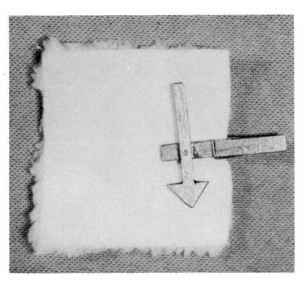

Figure 41. Method of marking pile line on fur fabric using a spring type wooden clothes peg and wooden arrow

marking the pile line is to obtain a wooden clip clothes-peg; cut out an arrow in card or wood and glue it across the peg (see figure 41), and clip this to the edge of the fabric.

Take care when placing the pattern pieces on the fur fabric backing that you keep the arrows on the pattern pieces lined up with the marked pile line. It is always advisable to avoid the soft selvedge edge of the fabric, so lay your pattern pieces on to the fabric away from the soft edge (this is usually only about 2.5cm [1in] in from the side).

Be aware of limbs which will require second halves and reverse pattern pieces accordingly. Never cut on the fold. Check the type of backing on your fabric, whether it is firm or stretchy, as this will affect the method of stuffing, jointing and fixing of eyes. If the backing is very soft, it may require additional fabric to the areas where the eyes may be placed.

Always draw round the pattern pieces with a soft pencil or, in the case of a dark coloured fabric, use tailor's chalk. Never use ballpoint pens as these will stain the fabric. Mark annotations on to each pattern piece, for example 'tail – cut one'. 'Cut a pair' means a left and a right piece, which is achieved by turning the pattern piece over to obtain the second half. This may also be written 'cut two – one reversed'. 'Cut two' on its own means to cut two exactly the same, i.e. duplicate pieces.

When cutting the fur fabric use the points of the scissors and cut the backing only – this avoids cutting and spoiling the pile. As you cut, the scissors then slide through the material backing and part any pile with which the scissors come into contact. Never turn the

scissors at angles, but turn the fabric to the scissors. When pinning the cut out fabric pieces together, push all the pile inside leaving a smooth outside edge with no pile caught between.

Choose thread that matches the fur fabric and use backstitch for stitching the pieces together and ladder stitching for applying ears etc., and closing openings.

After stitching and stuffing carefully, use a teazle brush or large sewing needle to pull out any pile caught in the seams. If care was taken at the pinning and stitching stages there should be very little pile to release.

Handling materials

These should be well pressed prior to cuting out.

Calico
Excellent for doll making as it is firm, strong and washable. It is preferable to wash and dry it first as this makes it easier to put a needle through. Calico can be dyed with a tea-bag.

Felt
Very easy and colourful to use for toymaking, it is always more satisfactory to have the stretch going across the toy. It is usually stitched on the right side with a small running stitch, or stab stitched.

Hessian
Always cut on the bias. It is advisable to stitch along the seam line and back again to form a double row of stitching.

Stockinette
This is easier to cut out after stitching, and is excellent for toys where needle-modelling is required. Great care should be taken at the stuffing stage as this material tends to stretch, though Iron-on Vilene will give it body.

Velvets
These are usually machine stitched or hand backstitched.

Courtelle fleece
A very useful material for toymaking as it has a firm texture with a soft fleece pile; the use of machine stitching is advisable. This material can be used for the smaller toy subjects for which ordinary fur fabric would be too bulky.

Jointing, wiring and specialist techniques

There are many methods and techniques which are covered in detail in *The Techniques of Soft Toymaking*, so it would not be applicable to use valuable pattern space by repeating the various processes here.

Safety designing

All the toy patterns in this book are designed to a high safety level. How does a new toymaker know what constitutes a safe toy? It is one that carefully takes into consideration all aspects of the mental and physical development, age and temperament of the child for whom the toy is being made.

Problems mainly occur when a toy is given to a child for whom it was not intended, or for whom it was not designed. One cannot generalise about which toys are suitable for any particular age group, as within such a group could be many differentials. It is much safer to choose a toy pattern that is suitable for the recipient.

Many toymakers, for example those selling toys commercially, never know the recipients of their toys; therefore all toys should be made to a high safety level, thus removing many safety problems.

APPENDIX III

CRAFT SUPPLIERS

U.K.

All toymaking materials are available from Granary Crafts, Bookham, Surrey (Furmofelt stockist).

Toy joints, bells, squeakers, chimes, growls

MARGRAVE MANUFACTURING CO. LTD,
MARGRAVE WORKS,
LONDON
SW6 4TJ

Fur fabrics, toy fillings

FLUFFY FABRICS,
UNIT N1/N2 TRIBUNE DRIVE,
TRINITY TRADING ESTATE
SITTINGBOURNE,
KENT

Comprehensive stockist of toymaking requirements

FRED ALDOUS LTD,
P.O. BOX 135,
37 LEVER STREET,
MANCHESTER
M60 1UX

Doll wigs and many toymaking requirements

MAIL ORDER DEPT.,
THE HANDICRAFT SHOP,
47 NORTHGATE,
CANTERBURY,
KENT
CT1 1BE

A range of good quality toy fillings

SAFLON LTD,
SAFFRON WAY,
LEICESTER
LE2 6UP

Musical movements (all types)

W. HOBBY LTD,
KNIGHTS HILL SQUARE,
LONDON
SE27 0HH

Funtex and all Vilene products

THE VILENE ORGANISATION,
P.O. BOX NO.3,
GREETLAND,
HALIFAX,
WEST YORKSHIRE
HX4 8NJ

Catalogues are available from the above firms; it is advisable to send postage.

U.S.A.

ADVENTURES IN CRAFT INC.,
218 EAST 81st STREET,
NEW YORK
NY 10028

STANDARD DOLL CO.,
23-83 31st STREET,
LONG ISLAND CITY,
NY 11105

New Zealand

All craft supplies; classes also conducted

HANDICRAFT HOUSE,
37 ORANGA AVENUE,
ONEHUNGA,
AUCKLAND 6

Australia

CRAFT PLUS,
89 LATROBE TERRACE,
PADDINGTON 4064

INDEX